—FAUX—
TAXIDERMY
KNITS

15 WILD ANIMAL
KNITTING PATTERNS

—FAUX—
TAXIDERMY
KNITS

15 WILD ANIMAL
KNITTING PATTERNS

LOUISE WALKER

D&C
David and Charles
www.stitchcraftcreate.co.uk

CONTENTS

INTRODUCTION

I have always been surrounded by creatures. As a child I adored the panda family who took residence in my doll's house and between my sisters and I there were hundreds of plush toy animals. Even now, a collection of toy sheep peak though the mountains of yarn in my studio. I don't think you're ever too old to have a pinch of Neverland here and there. Once I had learnt to knit it was only a matter of time before these influences began appearing in my work. It started with foxes and before I knew it I had created a whole world of animal friends. I could never bring myself to own a real trophy animal head or touch a real mink stole in a vintage shop, but knitting my own representations of them allowed me to delight in these things in my own way. The patterns in this book reflect a life-long love of toys and an admiration for taxidermy.

Within these pages you'll find a hoard of wild things: from beasts to be worn with pride, to nestlings that'll preserve the warmth of your tea to critters to keep you company on those cold wintery nights. You may recognise a few faces, such as my Fox Stole and a baby version of my Badger Head (who I couldn't resist including). I've given each piece its own personality but feel free to experiment yourself. Try making the crocodile grumpy or the moose a little shocked.

There's something for everybody. Beginners can keep themselves warm with the quick knit Raccoon Hat or, if superstitious, the Lucky Rabbit's Foot. Along the way there will be plenty of help. Clear diagrams and explanations of techniques mean there are no excuses for not trying the intermediate creatures. The book is packed with amusing projects that knitters of all abilities will enjoy making (I know I certainly did!) because what's life without a few pheasants hanging in your kitchen or a mole making mounds in the doorway.

WEARABLES

FOX STOLE

SKILL LEVEL
INTERMEDIATE

No evening outfit is complete without a pedigree pelt as the ultimate glamorous accessory. Drape this faux fox fur stole over your shoulders to release the foxy lady within.

MATERIALS

A Stylecraft Life DK, Copper x 2 balls (326 yards/298 metres per 100g)

B Stylecraft Life DK, Cream x 1 ball (326 yards/298 metres per 100g)

C Stylecraft Life DK, Black x 1 ball (326 yards/298 metres per 100g)

US 6 (4mm) straight needles

½in (10mm) black plastic eyes x 2

½in (10mm) black plastic triangular nose x 1 (or another ½in [10mm] eye can work just as well)

DIMENSIONS

74⅖in x 4½in (189 x 12cm)

GAUGE (TENSION)

22 stitches x 30 rows to 4in (10cm) over st st

KNITTING TECHNIQUES

Intarsia

Backstitch

BODY

Using US 6 (4mm) straight needles and colour A, CO 60 sts.

Work 348 rows in st st.

Row 349 (dec) K2tog, k56, k2tog. (58 sts)

Row 350 P all sts.

Repeat the last 2 rows 14 times. (30 sts)

Work 8 rows in st st.

Row 387 (inc) Kfb, k to the last st, kfb. (32 sts)

Work 3 rows in st st.

Row 391 (inc) Kfb, k to the last st, kfb. (34 sts)

Work 5 rows in st st.

Row 397 (dec) K2tog, k30, k2tog. (32 sts)

Work 3 rows in st st.

Row 401 (dec) K2tog, k to last st, k2tog. (30 sts)

Work 5 rows st st.

Row 407 (dec) K2tog, k to last 2 sts, k2tog. (28 sts)

Row 408 P all sts.

Repeat the last 2 rows 2 times. (24 sts)

Row 413 (dec) K3tog, k18, k3tog. (20 sts)

Row 414 P all sts.

Repeat the last 2 rows 2 times. (12 sts)

Row 419 (dec) K2tog, k8, k2tog. (10 sts)

Row 420 P all sts.

Work 10 rows in st st.

Change to colour B and work 10 more rows in st st.

Row 441 (inc) Kfb, k to last st, kfb. (12 sts)

Row 442 P all sts.

Row 443 (inc) Kfbf, k to last st, kfbf. (16 sts)

Row 444 P all sts.

Repeat the last 2 rows 2 times.

Row 449 (inc) Kfb, k to last st, kfb. (26 sts)

Row 450 P all sts.

Repeat the last 2 rows 2 times.

Work 4 rows in st st.

Row 459 (inc) Kfb, k28, kfb. (32 sts)

Work 3 rows in st st.

Row 463 (inc) Kfb, k30, kfb. (34 sts)

Work 5 rows in st st.

Row 469 (dec) K2tog, k30, k2tog. (32 sts)

Work 3 rows in st st.

Row 473 (dec) K2tog, k28, k2tog. (30 sts)

Work 9 rows in st st.

Row 483 (dec) K2tog, k to last st, k2tog. (28 sts)

Row 484 P all sts.

Repeat the last 2 rows until you have 4 sts.

Row 509 (dec) K2tog twice. (2 sts)

Row 510 P all sts.

Row 511 (dec) K2tog. (1 st)

Row 512 P all sts.

BO

LEGS

Make 4

Using US 6 (4mm) straight needles and colour A, CO 15 sts.

Work 64 rows in st st.

Change to colour C and continue working in st st to row 90.

Row 91 (dec) [K2tog] x7, k1.

Row 92 Cut the yarn and thread through the last 8 sts, pulling the yarn tight to shape the bottom of the foot.

EARS

Make 4

Using US 6 (4mm) straight needles and colour A, CO 16 sts.

Starting with a k row, work 10 rows in st st.

Row 11 (dec) K2tog, k to the last 2 sts, k2tog. (14 sts)

Row 12 P all sts.

Repeat the last 2 rows until you have 4 sts.

Row 23 (dec) [K2tog] x2. (2 sts)

BO purlwise.

TAIL

Using US 6 (4mm) straight needles and colour A, CO 15 sts.

Row 1 K all sts.

Row 2 P all sts.

Row 3 (inc) Kfb, k13, kfb. (17 sts)

Work 3 rows in st st.

Row 7 (inc) Kfb, k15, kfb. (19 sts)

Work 3 rows in st st.

Row 11 (inc) Kfb, k17, kfb. (21 sts)

Work 3 rows in st st.

Row 15 (inc) Kfb, k19, kfb. (23 sts)

Work 5 rows in st st.

Row 21 (inc) Kfb, k21, kfb. (25 sts)

Work 5 rows in st st.

Row 27 (inc) Kfb, k23, kfb. (27 sts)

Work 5 rows in st st.

Row 33 (inc) Kfb, k25, kfb. (29 sts)

Work 7 rows in st st.

Row 41 (inc) Kfb, k27, kfb. (31 sts)

Work 7 rows in st st.

Row 49 (inc) Kfb, k29, kfb. (33 sts)

Work 7 rows in st st.

Row 57 (inc) Kfb, k31, kfb. (35 sts)

Work 9 rows in st st.

Row 67 Change to colour B and work in st st to row 98.

Row 99 (dec) K3tog, k to the last 3 sts, k3tog. (31 sts)

Row 100 P all sts.

Repeat the last 2 rows until you have 7 sts, ending in a p row.

Row 113 (dec) [K2tog] x3, k1. (4 sts)

Row 114 Cut the yarn and thread through the last 4 sts, pulling the yarn tight to shape the bottom of the tail.

TO MAKE YOUR FOX LONGER OR SHORTER, ADD OR SUBTRACT ROWS IN THE BODY SECTION

SEWING UP

BODY

Block your fox. Weave in the ends. Fold the body in half, with the right side (RS) facing inwards, and pin along the seam to the start of the decrease. Then lay flat with the pinned seam in the middle of the stole facing up.

When sewing up the fox, the end of the nose needs to be folded with the RS facing in. The fold needs be placed where the earlier colour change was made. Pin both sides. The cream decrease will match the triangular shape on the decrease of the copper.

Then, using backstitch (see Techniques), sew up the middle seam and the two seams from the decrease to the end of the nose. Leave the tail end open and turn the piece inside out.

LEGS

Fold the legs in half, with the RS facing inwards, and pin along the seam. Starting with the black yarn that was pulled tight, sew along the leg. Change to copper yarn once the black section is sewn up. Leave the cast-on (CO) edge open and then turn inside out. The seam will form at the back.

TAIL

Fold the tail in half, with the RS facing inward, and pin along the seam. Starting with the cream yarn that was pulled tight, sew along the tail. Change to copper yarn once the cream yarn is sewn up. Leave the CO edge open and then turn inside out. The seam will form at the back.

EARS

Place the two panels against each other, RS facing inward, pin the two side seams, leaving the CO edge open. Sew up and turn inside out. Repeat for the second ear.

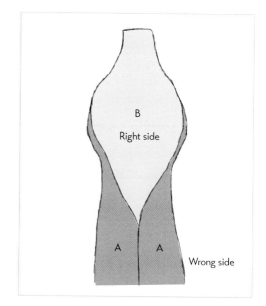

MAKING UP

FACE

Find the middle of the nose. Use pins to vertically mark 4½in (12cm) along the face. Measure 3in (7.5cm) from the nose and four stitches left of the centre pin markers, place and secure the left eye here. Repeat for the right eye (measuring four stitches right of the centre pin marker). Place the nose in the centre of the bottom of the face, two stitches up from the start of the copper. Then measure 4½ in (11cm) from the nose and two stitches left of the centre pin marker, mark this with a new pin. Place the left ear between the edge of the face and the new marker, and pin the ear down. Repeat for the right ear (marking two stitches right of the centre pin marker). Carefully sew the ears in place, then remove the pin markers. Add a couple of stitches at the back of the ears, in the centre, these will push the ears back slightly so they do not droop forwards.

FRONT LEGS

Turn the fox and lay flat, with the body seam facing up and in the centre. Place the left leg so that the start of the black meets with the end of the nose. Pin the leg 9in (21cm) up from this point, on the edge of the body. It will sit on the copper decrease. Repeat for the other leg on the right side of the body. Then sew the legs in place, adding an extra three stitches down the leg at small intervals. This will hold the legs straight.

BACK LEGS AND TAIL

Lay the piece flat, again, ensure the body seam is dead centre. Start by pinning the centre seam side of the left leg onto the left edge of the back of the fox. Do the same to the right leg. Match the back of the tail seam to the centre body seam and pin. Pin the front of the pieces together. Then sew up all three using the copper yarn. There will be two small gaps between the tail and either leg. Sew these up.

HEDGEHOG SLIPPERS

SKILL LEVEL
INTERMEDIATE

These Hedgehog Slippers use tweedy picot edging and luxurious chunky yarn on the base. They are fantastic fun and so cosy and comfortable to wear, perfect for whiling away those cold winter evenings with some knitting in front of the fire!

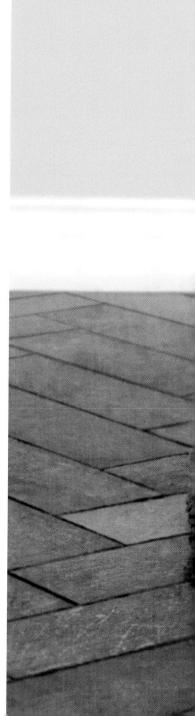

MATERIALS

A Stylecraft, Special Double Knit, Camel x 1 ball (332 yards/294 metres per 100g)

B Texere Yarns, Troon Tweed, Terracotta & Rust x 3 balls (186 yards/170 metres per 100g)

C Texere Yarns, Plush Chenille, Truffle x 2 balls (120 yards/110 metres per 100g)

US 6 (4mm) straight needles

US 6 (4mm) DPNs

US 8 (5mm) DPNs

US 8 (5mm) straight needles

1oz (25g) toy stuffing per slipper

Hedgehog eyes and nose template (see Templates)

½ x ¾in (1 x 2cm) black felt for each eye and 1 x 1in (2.5 x 2.5cm) for the nose

DIMENSIONS

11 x 5 x 5½in (29 x 13 x 14cm)

GAUGE (TENSION)

20 sts and 30 rows to 4in (10cm) over st st on US 6 (4mm) needles.

19 sts and 24 rows to 4in (10cm) over st st on US 8 (5mm) needles

KNITTING TECHNIQUES

Long-tail cast on

SLIPPER SOLE

Make 4

Using the long-tail CO method (see Techniques) and US 6 (4mm) straight needles, CO 5 sts in colour C. This will make up the 1st row.

Row 2 K all sts.

Row 3 (inc) Kfb across all sts. (10st)

Row 4–28 Work in garter st.

Row 29 (inc) K1, kfb, k6, kfb, k1. (12 sts)

Row 30 K all sts.

Row 31 K all sts.

Row 32 K all sts.

Row 33 K all sts.

Row 34 K all sts.

Row 35 (inc) K1, kfb, k8, kfb, k1. (14 sts)

Row 36–46 Work in garter st.

Row 47 (dec) K1, ssk, k8, k2tog, k1. (12 sts)

Row 48 K all sts.

Row 49 (dec) K1, ssk, k6, k2tog, k1. (10 sts)

Row 50 K all sts.

Row 51 (dec) K1, ssk, k4, k2tog, k1. (8 sts)

Row 52 K all sts.

Row 53 (dec) K1, ssk, k2, k2tog, k1. (6 sts)

Row 54 K all sts.

BO

SOLE EDGE

Using the long-tail CO method (see Techniques) and US 6 (4mm) straight needles, CO 81 sts in colour C. This will make up the 1st row. Be careful not to CO too loosely as this may effect the size of the edge, which will make sewing up harder.

Row 2 P all sts.

Row 3 K all sts.

Row 4 P all sts.

Row 5 K all sts.

Row 6 P all sts.

BO

HEDGEHOG

Make 2

Using the long-tail CO method (see Techniques) and US 6 (4mm) DPNs, CO 6 sts in colour A. This will make up the 1st round.

Row 2 K all sts.

Row 3 (inc) Kfb across all sts. (12 sts)

Row 4 K all sts.

Row 5 (inc) *Kfb, k1* repeat from * to end. (18 sts)

Row 6 K all sts.

Row 7 K all sts.

Row 8 (inc) *Kfb, k2* repeat from * to end. (24 sts)

Row 9 K all sts.

Row 10 K all sts.

Row 11 K all sts.

Row 12 K all sts.

Row 13 K all sts.

Row 14 K all sts.

Row 15 (inc) *Kfb, k3* repeat from * to end. (30 sts)

Row 16 K all sts.

Row 17 (inc) *Kfb, k4* repeat from * to end. (36 sts)

Row 18 K all sts.

Row 19 K all sts.

Row 20 K all sts.

Row 21 K all sts.

Row 22 K all sts.

Row 23 K all sts.

Row 24 Change to colour B and US 8 (5mm) DPNs and k all sts.

Row 25 (inc) *Kfb, k1* repeat from * to end. (54 sts)

Row 26 K all sts.

Row 27 K all sts.

Row 28 BO 18 sts, k across the remaining 36 sts.

Row 29 Change to US 8 (5mm) straight needles and slip the 1st st *yo, k2tog* repeat from * to end, k1.

Work 11 rows in st st.

Row 41 S1, *yo, k2tog* until the last st, k1. (36 sts)

Repeat rows 30–41, 11 more times to row 173.

Row 174 K all sts.

Row 175 P all sts.

Row 176 K all sts.

Row 177 P all sts.

Row 178 K all sts.

Row 179 P all sts.

RIGHT SIDE OF ANKLE

Row 180 K18, place the remaining sts on a stitch holder.

Row 181 BO 1 st purlwise, p to end. (17 sts)

Row 182 K all sts.

Row 183 BO 1 st purlwise, p to end. (16 sts)

Row 184 K all sts.

Row 185 BO 1 purlwise, *yo, k2tog* repeat from * to end. (15 sts)

Row 186 K all sts.

Row 187 BO 1 st purlwise, p to end. (14 sts)

Work 9 rows in st st.

Row 197 S1, [yo, k2tog] x 6, k1.

Work 6 rows in st st.

Repeat rows 192–203, 6 times to row 263.

Row 264 K all sts.

Row 265 P all sts.

BO

LEFT SIDE OF ANKLE

Row 180 (inc) Pick up the 18 sts placed on stitch holder at row 180. K2tog, k to end. (17 sts)

Row 181 P all sts.

Row 182 (dec) K2tog, k to the end. (16 sts)

Row 183 P all sts.

Row 184 (dec) K2tog, k to the end. (15 sts)

Row 185 S1, *yo, k2tog* repeat from * to end. (15 sts)

Row 186 (dec) K2tog, k to the end. (14 sts)

Row 187 P all sts.

Work 9 rows in st st.

Row 197 S1, [yo, k2tog] x 6, k1.

Work 6 rows in st st.

Repeat rows 192–203, 6 times to row 263.

Row 264 K all sts.

Row 265 P all sts.

BO

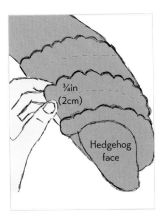

¾in (2cm)

Hedgehog face

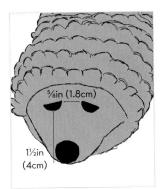

⅝in (1.8cm)

1½in (4cm)

MAKING UP

FINISHING THE SOLES

Make 2

Take 1 of the soles and pin the sole edge around it with the knit side facing up. Start at the bottom of the sole and stitch up using colour C. Once this is sewn, place the 2nd sole on top of the sole edge (with the purl side facing in). Repeat the process for the bottom piece, but leave a small gap. Turn inside out and add the stuffing evenly. Then neatly sew up the hole.

HEDGEHOG TOP

Make 2

Starting from the top of the hedgehog (from the face) take the 1st picot edge and fold, creating the spikes. Pin together and, using a small and careful st, sew ¾in (2cm) under the spike using colour B (running through the front and back of the fold). Repeat for every picot edge.

With every edge sewn, starting from the beginning again, pin the 1st and 2nd edge together. Sew the 2 together with colour B (being very careful to make the sts invisible). Sew all picot edges together.

There will be an extra amount of st st on the last picot edge Sew this onto the back of the edge on both sides. And then sew the 2 back pieces securely together.

Then place the top of the hedgehog onto the base and pin. The BO bottom of the hedgehog will sit on the front of the base with the seam on the base and the seam of the picot edge meeting. Sew securely using colour B.

Cut out 2 black felt eyes and one nose using the templates (see Templates). Using black cotton sew the nose onto the top of the face in the centre and the eyes 1½in (4cm) from the CO edge with ⅝in (1.8cm) between them.

WHEN SEWING THE PICOT EDGING TOGETHER MAKE SURE YOU USE COLOUR B TO MAKE THE STITCHES AS INVISIBLE AND SECURE AS POSSIBLE.

RACCOON HAT

SKILL LEVEL
BEGINNER

The iconic Raccoon Hat is more often associated with wild frontiers and Davy Crockett-type characters. The beauty of this one is that you can sleep easy knowing that no raccoons were harmed in the making of this hat!

MATERIALS

A Erika Knight, Fur Wool, Milk Chocolate x 3 balls
(44 yards/40 metres per 100g)

B Erika Knight , Fur Wool, Pitch x 1 ball
(44 yards/40 metres per 100g)

US 15 (10mm) needles

Wadding 5½in (14cm) x by 23 ⅝ in (60cm) for the band
and a square 23 ⅝ in (60cm) piece for the top of the hat.

DIMENSIONS

HAT: 10 ½ x 6 ¼in (26 x 16cm)
TAIL: 9½in (24cm)

GAUGE (TENSION)

5 sts and 10 rows to 4in (10cm) over st st

KNITTING TECHNIQUES

Long-tail cast on

Mattress stitch

BAND

Using the long-tail CO method (see Techniques) and
US 15 (10mm) needles, CO 36 sts in colour A. Work in
garter st until the piece measures 12in (30cm).

TOP OF THE HAT

Make 2

Using the long-tail CO method (see Techniques) and
US 15 (10mm) needles, CO 50 sts in A. This will make
up the 1st row.

Row 2 (dec) *K2tog, k3* repeat from * to end. (40 sts)

Row 3 K all sts.

Row 4 (dec) *K2tog, k2* repeat from * to end. (30 sts)

Row 5 K all sts.

Row 6 (dec) *K2tog, k1* repeat from * to end. (20 sts)

Row 7 K all sts.

Row 8 (dec) K2tog across all sts. (10 sts)

Row 9 K all sts.

Row 10 (dec) K2tog across all sts. (5 sts)

Break yarn, leaving a long tail, thread through remaining live
sts and pull through. Weave in ends.

USE WADDING OR EVENLY STUFF THE HAT WITH
FLAT TOY STUFFING. THIS WILL SHAPE THE HAT AND
ALSO KEEP YOU EXTRA SNUG.

TAIL

Using the long-tail CO method (see Techniques) and US 15 (10mm) needles, CO 10 sts in colour A. This will make up the 1st row.

Row 2–6 K all sts.

Row 7 Change to colour B and k all sts.

Row 8 K all sts.

Row 9 Change to colour A and k all sts.

Row 10 K all sts.

Row 11 Change to color B and k all sts.

Row 12 K all sts.

Row 13 Change to colour A and k all sts.

Row 14 K all sts.

Row 15 Change to colour B and k all sts.

Row 16 K all sts.

Row 17 (dec) Change to colour A. [K2tog, k1] x 3, k2. (7 sts)

Row 18 K all sts.

Row 19 Change to colour B and k all sts.

Row 20 K all sts.

Row 21 Change to colour A and k all sts.

Row 22 K all sts.

Row 23 (dec) [K2tog] x 3, k1. (4 sts)

Row 24 K all sts.

Break yarn, leaving a long tail, thread through the sts and pull.

ADD A FEW EXTRA STRIPES TO THE TAIL IF YOU
WANT TO MAKE IT LONGER.

MAKING UP

Fold the tail so the stripes match up, with the RS facing in. Sew up using mattress stitch (see Techniques), leaving the CO edge open.

Taking the band, place the strip of wadding into it, fold so the CO and BO edge meet. Pin together and sew, joining the garter stitch, pin and sew the short ends of the bands. Place both short ends together, pin and sew. This will create the band of the hat.

Take both tops of the knitted hats. The hats will form a circle with a seam that needs sewing up. Join the garter stitch together to sew the seam on both pieces of the hat. Cut the square wadding to match the top circle piece. Then place between the two pieces and join up.

Place the top piece onto the band and securely sew together. The folded edge of the band should be the piece that is sewn into.

Pin the tail onto the bottom of the back of the hat, you can choose where you'd like it to sit. Here I've chosen to place it a quarter of the way around from the left of the seam.

LUCKY RABBIT'S FOOT

SKILL LEVEL
BEGINNER

This is a cute take on the ancient belief that a rabbit's foot brings the carrier good luck. So, my advice to you is attach this simple knit to your purse or bag to bring good fortune to all your endeavours!

MATERIALS

Drops, Alpaca Silk, Light Beige 1 x 50g ball (153 yards/140 metres per 50g)

Bergere De France, Angel, Blanc Casse 1 x 25g ball (300 yards/275 metres per 25g)

A small amount of brown aran yarn, such as the Malabrigo, Rich Chocolate or Sincerely Louise, Moose

US 6 (4mm) DPNs

6 inch silver/metal ball chain ¹⁄₁₆in (2mm) thickness

Antique silver dome bead cap ½ x ³⁄₈in (10 x 8mm) with ³⁄₈in (8mm) inner diametre

¼in (5mm) silver tone jump ring

Small pliers

Multipurpose fabric glue

A handful of toy stuffing

DIMENSIONS

1⅜ x 2¾in (3.5 x 7cm)

GAUGE (TENSION)

23 sts and 28 rows to 4in (10cm) over st st

KNITTING TECHNIQUES

Long-tail cast on

RABBIT'S FOOT

Using the long-tail CO method (see Techniques) and US 6 (4mm) needles CO 6 sts and split across three DPNs. This will make up the 1st row.

Row 2 K all sts.

Row 3 (inc) *Kfb* all sts. (12 sts)

Row 4 K all sts.

Row 5 (inc) *Kfb, K1* repeat from * to end. (18 sts)

Work 13 rows in st st.

Row 19 (dec) *K2tog, K1* repeat from * to end. (12 sts)

At this point you need to stuff the foot, be careful not to over stuff!

Row 20 (dec) *K2tog * repeat from * to end. (6 sts)

Row 21 (dec) *K2tog across all sts. (3 sts)

Row 22 BO, leaving a long tail of thread.

MAKING UP

Wrap the tail of thread around the small tube made by the BO edge, wrap about ³⁄₈in (8mm) down, pull tight and sew in.

Neatly sew in the CO yarn, pulling tight.

Using the pliers, open up the ¼in (5mm) jump ring and thread into the small hole on the top of the bead cap. Then thread a link of the ball chain into the jump ring. Close up using the pliers.

Take the bead cap, and fill with fabric glue ¾ of the way up. Then place onto the top of the foot. Hold in place for a minute. Leave to dry.

Take a small amount of brown aran yarn and sew onto the rabbit's foot. Sew three small lines, approximately ⅝in (1.5cm) long.

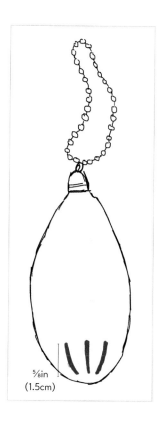

⅝in (1.5cm)

TRY CHANGING THE TWO
STRANDS OF COLOURS TO MAKE
ENDLESS VARIATIONS OF THESE
RABBIT FEET.

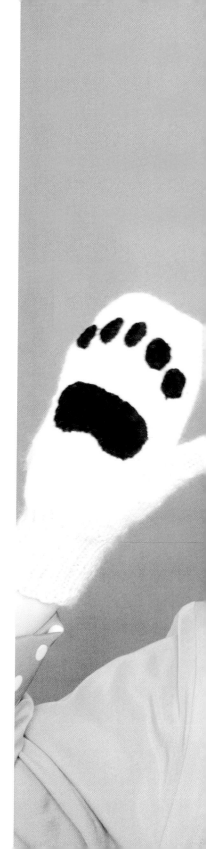

POLAR BEAR PAW MITTENS

SKILL LEVEL
INTERMEDIATE

If you go down to the woods today be sure to wear these

cosy Polar Bear Paw Mittens. Made from the softest yarn,

they are the perfect woolly cover up for chilly days. Wear

them with pride and they are certain to protect you from

any grisly encounters!

MATERIALS

A Wool and the Gang, Baby Alpaca, Snow White x 2 balls (127 yards/116 metres per 50g)

B Wool and the Gang, Baby Alpaca, Midnight Blue x 1 ball (127 yards/116 metres per 50g)

US 2 (3mm) DPNs

US 4 (3.5mm) DPNs

Stitch holder

DIMENSIONS

13 x 5in (33 x 13.5cm)

GAUGE (TENSION)

24 sts x 30 rows to 4in (10cm) over st st

KNITTING TECHNIQUES

Long-tail cast on

Intarsia

RIGHT HAND

Using the long-tail CO method (see Techniques) and US 2 (3mm) DPNs CO 44 sts in colour A. Join to work in the round. This will make up the 1st round.

Round 2 *P2, k2* repeat from * to end.

Round 3–21 Repeat round 2.

Round 22 (inc) Change to US 4 (3.5mm) DPNs. *Kfb, k3* repeat from * to end. (55 sts)

Round 23 K all sts.

Round 24 K all sts.

Round 25 (inc) K27, m1, k1, m1, k27. (57 sts)

Round 26 K all sts.

Round 27 K all sts.

Round 28 K all sts.

Round 29 K all sts.

Round 30 (inc) K27, m1, k3, m1, k27. (59 sts)

Round 31 K all sts.

Round 32 K all sts.

Round 33 K all sts.

Round 34 K all sts.

Round 35 (inc) K27, m1, k5, m1, k27. (61 sts)

Round 36 K all sts.

Round 37 K all sts.

Round 38 K38a, k6b, k7a, k6b, k4a.

Round 39 K37a, k8b, k5a, k8b, k3a.

Round 40 (inc) K27a, m1a, k7a, m1a, k2a, k10b, k3a, k10b, k2a. (63 sts)

Round 41 K38a, k23b, k2a.

Repeat the last round three times.

Round 45 (inc) K27a, m1a, k9a, m1a, k2a, k23b, k2a. (65 sts)

Round 46 K41a, k21b, k3a.

Round 47 K42a, k19b, k4a.

Round 48 K43a, k17b, k5a.

Round 49 K44a, k15b, k6a.

Round 50 K27a, Place 11 sts on a stitch holder, k7a, k13b, k7a. (54 sts)

Round 51 (inc) [Kfb, k10] x 3 in colour A, kfba, k1a, k9b, kfb in b, k1b, k8a. (59 sts)

Round 52 K41a, k8b, k10a.

Round 53 K all sts in colour A.

Round 54 (inc) [Kfb, k11] x 5, k10. (64 sts)

Round 55 K all sts.

Round 56 K all sts.

Round 57 K all sts.

Round 58 K all sts.

Round 59 K all sts.

Round 60 K all sts.

Round 61 K35a, k3b, k21a, k3b, k2a.

Round 62 K34a, k5b, k19a, k5b, k1a.

Round 63 K all sts.

Round 64 K all sts.

Round 65 K35a, k3b, k2a, k3b, k11a, k3b, k2a, k3b, k2a.

Round 66 K39a, k5b, k9a, k5b, k6a.

Round 67 K all sts.

Round 68 K39a, k5b, k3a, k3b, k3a, k5b, k6a.

Round 69 K39a, k5b, k2a, k5b, k2a, k5b, k6a.

Round 70 K40a, k3b, k3a, k5b, k3a, k3b, k7a.

Round 71 K46a, k5b, k13a.

Round 72 K47a, k3b, k14a.

Round 73 K all sts in colour A.

Round 74 K all sts.

Round 75 K all sts.

Round 76 (dec) *K2tog, k5* repeat from * to end. (54 sts)

Round 77 (dec) *K2tog, k4* repeat from * to end. (46 sts)

Round 78 (dec) *K2tog, k3* repeat from * to end. (38 sts)

Round 79 (dec) *K2tog, k2* repeat from * to end. (30 sts)

Round 81 (dec) *K2tog, k1* repeat from * to end. (22 sts)

Round 82 (dec) K2tog to end. (14 sts)

Round 83 (dec) K2tog to end. (7 sts)

Break yarn, leaving a long tail, thread through remaining live sts and pull through. Weave in ends.

YOU CAN EITHER CARRY THE COLOUR OR CUT AND RE-START THE YARN EACH TIME.

LEFT HAND

Using the long-tail CO method (see Techniques) and US 2 (3mm) DPNs CO 44 sts in colour A. Join to work in the round. This will make up the 1st round.

Round 2 *P2, k2* repeat from * to end.

Round 3–21 repeat round 2.

Round 22 (inc) Change to US 4 (3.5mm) DPNS. *Kfb, k3* repeat from * to end. (55 sts)

Round 23 K all sts.

Round 24 K all sts.

Round 25 (inc) K27, m1, k1, m1, K27. (57 sts)

Round 26 K all sts.

Round 27 K all sts.

Round 28 K all sts.

Round 29 K all sts.

Round 30 (inc) K27, m1, k3, m1, k27. (59 sts)

Round 31 K all sts.

Round 32 K all sts.

Round 33 K all sts.

Round 34 K all sts.

Round 35 (inc) K27, m1, k5, m1, k27. (61 sts)

Round 36 K all sts.

Round 37 K all sts.

Round 38 K4a, k6b, k7a, k6b, k38a.

Round 39 K3a, k8b, k5a, k8b, k37a.

Round 40 K2a, k10b, k3a, k10b, k2a, m1a, k7a, m1a, k27a. (63 sts)

Round 41 K2A, k23b, k38a.

Repeat the last round three times.

Round 45 (inc) k2a, k23b, k2a, m1a, k9a, m1a, k27a. (65 sts)

Round 46 K3a, k21b, k41a.

Round 47 K4a, k19b, k42a.

Round 48 K5a, k17b, k43a.

Round 49 K6a, k15b, k44a.

Round 50 K7a, k13b, k7a, Place 11 sts on a stitch holder. (54 sts)

Round 51 (inc) K8a, k1b, kfb in b, k9b, k1a, kfb in a, [k10, kfb] x 3a. (59 sts)

Round 52 K10a, k8b, k41a.

Round 53 K all sts in colour A.

Round 54 (inc) K10, [k11, kfb] x 5. (64 sts)

Round 55 K all sts.

Round 56 K all sts.

Round 57 K all sts.

Round 58 K all sts.

Round 59 K all sts.

Round 60 K all sts

Round 61 K2a, k3b, k21a, k3b, k35a.

Round 62 K1a, k5b, k19a, k5b, k34a.

Round 63 K all sts.

Round 64 K all sts.

Round 65 K2a, k3b, k2a, k11a, k3b, k2a, k3b, k35a.

Round 66 K6a, k5b, k9a, k5b, k39a.

Round 67 K all sts.

Round 68 K6a, k5b, k3a, k3b, k3a, k5b, k39a.

Round 69 K6b, k5b, k2a, k5b, k2a, k5b, k39a.

Round 70 K7a, k3b, k3a, k5b, k3a, k3b, k40a.

Round 71 K13a, k5b, k46a.

Round 72 K14a, k3b, k47a.

Round 73 K all sts in colour A.

Round 74 K all sts.

Round 75 K all sts.

Round 76 (dec) *K2tog, k5* repeat from * to end. (54 sts)

Round 77 (dec) *K2tog, k4* repeat from * to end. (46 sts)

Round 78 (dec) *K2tog, k3* repeat from * to end. (38 sts)

Round 79 (dec) *K2tog, k2* repeat from * to end. (30 sts)

Round 81 (dec) *K2tog, k1* repeat from * to end. (22 sts)

Round 82 (dec) K2tog to end. (14 sts)

Round 83 (dec) K2tog to end. (7 sts)

Break the yarn, leaving a long tail, thread through remaining live stitches and pull through. Weave in ends.

THUMBS

Pick up the 11 stitches on stitch holder. Pick up two stitches extra on either side of the mitten. Split the 15 stitches evenly over three US 4 (3.5mm) DPNs.

Work 16 rounds in st st.

Round 17 (dec) *K2tog, k1* repeat from * to end. (10 sts)

Round 18 (dec) K2tog to end. (5 sts)

Break the yarn, leaving a long tail, thread through remaining live stitches and pull through. Weave in ends.

MAKING UP

PAWS

Using the black yarn, embroider around all the edges of the stitches made in colour B. Simply blend short black lines into the edges for ¼in (5mm) or so. This will neaten up the piece and puff out the black, which gives the mittens that real polar bear feel.

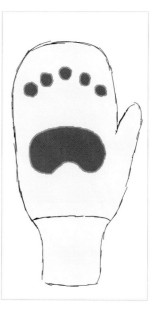

GO WILD EMBROIDERING AROUND THE EDGES, RAISING THE BLACK WILL MAKE THE MITTENS NEATER AND MAKE THEM FEEL LIKE REAL POLAR BEAR PAWS!

MINK WRAP

SKILL LEVEL
BEGINNER

If you're looking for some 1940s-style glamour then

look no further. This opulent, hand-crafted Mink Wrap

will complement your outfit with elegant charm!

MATERIALS

A Malabrigo, Worsted, Rich Chocolate x 2 balls
(210 yards/192 metres per 100g)

B Malabrigo, Merino Worsted, Marroon Oscuro x 1 ball
(210 yards/192 metres per 100g)

C Malabrigo, Merino Worsted, Applewood x 1 ball
(210 yards/192 metres per 100g)

US 8 (5mm) straight needles

½in (10mm) toy eyes x 3

1 fur hook and eye, beige

DIMENSIONS

35 x 4½in (90 x 12cm)

GAUGE (TENSION)

18 sts and 26 rows to 4in (10cm) over st st

KNITTING TECHNIQUES

Long-tail cast on

Intarsia

Mattress stitch

TOP OF MINK

Make 2

Using the long-tail CO method
(see Techniques) and US 8 (5mm)
needles CO 4 sts in colour A. This will
make up the 1st row.

Row 2 P all sts.

Row 3 K all sts.

Row 4 P all sts.

Row 5 (inc) Kfb, k2, kfb. (6 sts)

Row 6 P all sts.

Row 7 K all sts.

Row 8 P all sts.

Row 9 (inc) Kfb, k4, kfb. (8 sts)

Row 10 P all sts.

Row 11 K all sts.

Row 12 P all sts.

Row 13 (inc) Kfb, k6, kfb. (10 sts)

Row 14 P all sts.

Row 15 (inc) *Kfb, k1* repeat from *
to end. (15 sts)

Row 16 P all sts.

Row 17 (inc) *Kfb, k2* repeat from *
to end. (20 sts)

Row 18 P all sts.

Row 19 (inc) *Kfb, k3* repeat from *
to end. (25 sts)

Row 20 P all sts.

Row 21 K1c, k23a, k1c.

Row 22 P1c, p23a, p1c.

Repeat the last 2 rows, 2 times.

Row 27 (inc) Kfb in colour C, k23a,
kfb in colour C. (27 sts)

Row 28 P2c, p23a, p2c.

Row 29 K2c, k10a, k3b, k10a, k2c.

Row 30 P2c, p10a, p3b, p10a, p2c.

Repeat the last 2 rows.

Row 33 K2c, k9a, k5b, k9a, k2c.

Row 34 P2c, p9a, p5b, p9a, p2c.

Repeat the last 2 rows.

Row 37 K2c, k8a, k7b, k8a, k2c.

Row 38 P2c, p8a, p7b, p8a, p7b,
p2c.

Row 39 K3c, k7a, k7b, k7a, k3c.

Row 40 P3c, p7a, p7b, p7a, p3c.

Repeat the last 2 rows, 2 times.

Row 45 K3c, k8a, k5b, k8a, k3c.

Row 46 P3c, p8a, p5b, p8a, p3c.

Row 47 K3c, k8a, k5b, k8a, k3c.

Row 48 P3c, p8a, p5b, p8a, p3c.

Row 49 K3c, k8a, k5b, k8a, k3c.

Row 50 P3c, p8a, p5b, p8a, p3c.

Row 51 K3c, k8a, k5b, k8a, k3c.

Row 52 P3c, p8a, p5b, p8a, p3c.

Row 53 K3c, k8a, k5b, k8a, k3c.

Row 54 P3c, p8a, p5b, p8a, p3c.

Row 55 K3c, k8a, k5b, k8a, k3c.

Row 56 P3c, p8a, p5b, p8a, p3c.

Row 57 K3c, k7a, k7b, k7a, k3c.

Row 58 P3c, p7a, p7b, p7a, p3c.

Row 59 K3c, k7a, k7b, k7a, k3c.

Row 60 P3c, p7a, p7b, p7a, p3c.

Row 61 K3c, k7a, k7b, k7a, k3c.

Row 62 P3c, p7a, p7b, p7a, p3c.

Repeat rows 45–62, 6 more times to
row 170.

Row 171 K3c, k8a, k5b, k8a, k3c.

Row 172 P3c, p8a, p5b, p8a, p3c.

Repeat rows 171 and 172, 2 times more
to row 176.

Row 177 K3c, k7a, k7b, k7a, k3c.

Row 178 P3c, p6a, p9b, p6a, p3c.

Row 179 K3c, k5a, k11b, k5a, k3c.

Row 180 P3c, p4a, p13b, p4a, p3c.

Row 181 K3c, k3a, k15b, k3a, k3c.

Row 182 P3c, p2a, p17b, p2a, p3c.

Row 183 K2c, k2a, k19b, k2a, k2c.

Row 184 P2c, p1a, p21b, p1a, p2c.

Row 185 K2c, k23b, k2c.

Row 186 P2c, p23b, p2c.

Row 187 K1c, k25b, k1c.

Row 188 P all sts in colour B.

Row 189 BO in colour B.

BOTTOM OF MINK

Make 2

Using the long-tail CO method (see Techniques) and US 8 (5mm) needles CO 4 sts in colour A. This will make up the 1st row.

Work the pattern for Top of Mink until row 20.

Row 21–186 Work st st in colour A.

Row 187 Change to colour B and k all sts.

Row 188 P all sts.

BO

EARS

Make 4

Using the long-tail CO method (see Techniques)and US 8 (5mm) needles CO 5 sts in colour B. This will make up the 1st row.

Row 2 P all sts.

Row 3 K all sts.

Row 4 P all sts.

Row 5 (dec) K2tog, k1, k2tog. (3 sts)

Row 6 P all sts.

Row 7 (dec) K3tog across all sts.

Break yarn, leaving a long tail, and thread through remaining live sts. Weave in ends.

LEGS

Make 16

Using the long-tail CO method (see Techniques) and US 8 (5mm) needles CO 8 sts in colour B. This will make up the 1st row.

Row 2 P all sts.

Work 16 rows in st st.

Row 19 (dec) K2tog across all sts. (4 sts)

Break yarn, leaving a long tail, and thread through remaining live sts. Weave in ends.

TAILS

Make 4

Using the long-tail CO method (see Techniques) and US 8 (5mm) needles CO 12 sts in colour B. This will make up the 1st row.

Row 2 P all sts.

Row 3 (inc) *Kfb, k3* repeat from * to end. (15 sts)

Work 3 rows in st st.

Row 7 (inc) *Kfb, k4* repeat from * to end. (18 sts)

Row 8 P all sts.

Work 18 rows in st st.

Row 27 (dec) *K2tog, k4* repeat from * to end. (15 sts)

Row 28 P all sts.

Row 29 (dec) *K2tog, k3* repeat from * to end. (12 sts)

Row 30 P all sts.

Row 31 (dec) *K2tog, k2* repeat from * to end. (9 sts)

Row 32 P all sts.

Row 33 (dec) *K2tog, k1* repeat from * to end. (6 sts)

Break yarn, leaving a long tail, and thread through remaining live sts. Weave in ends.

MAKING UP

Block your mink. Weave in ends. Take a top piece and bottom piece of the mink, place them together with the RS facing in. Pin and sew up. Leave the BO edges open and turn the piece inside out.

EARS

Make 4

Take two ear pieces and place them together with the RS facing in, then sew up. Turn inside out.

TAILS

Make 2

Take two tail pieces and place them together with the RS facing in, then sew up. Turn inside out and repeat.

LEGS

Make 8

Take 2 leg pieces and place them together with the RS facing in, then sew up. Turn inside out.

FACE

Place two eyes 2¾in (7cm) from the start of the snout (the CO edge), leaving a ⅝in (1.5cm) gap between them, secure in place. Place the two ears 4in (10cm) from the start of the snout leaving a 1¾in (4.5cm) gap in the centre between them, sew them neatly into the mink using colour B. Place the nose in the centre of the base of the nose and secure in place.

Sew up the BO edge of the mink using mattress st (see Techniques) and colour B. Place two legs at the edges of the base of the mink. Place the tail in the centre of the edge, leaving a 1¾in (3.5cm) gap between the legs. Pin and sew the legs using colour B. Place two more legs on the edges of the top of the mink, 2¾in (7cm) from the base of the snout. Pin and secure using colour B.

ATTACHING THE HOOK AND EYE

The mink is fastened by a hook and eye. Place the eye 12in (30cm) from the BO edge of the front of one mink. It will sit just next to the line of the B colour change. The hook needs to be placed 2¾in (7cm) from the CO edge, on the underneath of the face and in the centre, and the eye 2¾in (7cm) from the CO edge (on the underneath and in the centre).

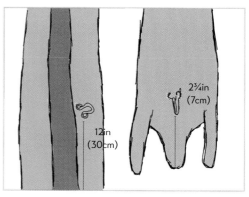

BE INVENTIVE, TRY WEARING YOUR MINK IN DIFFERENT WAYS, MAYBE EVEN KNIT A THIRD TO IMPRESS FRIENDS AT SOCIAL EVENTS.

WOLF
HEADDRESS

SKILL LEVEL
INTERMEDIATE

A feared and revered creature, the wolf symbolizes

freedom and intelligence – so why not channel your inner

wolf and turn a few heads this winter with this impressive

Wolf Headdress!

MATERIALS

A Rowan, Alpaca Cotton, Storm x 1 ball (148 yards/135 metres per 50g)

B Rowan, Alpaca Cotton, Raindrop x 1 ball (148 yards/135 metres per 50g)

C Rowan, Alpaca Cotton, Rice x 1 ball (148 yards/135 metres per 50g)

D Rowan, Purelife British Sheep Breeds Bouclé, Light Brown Masham x 2 balls (66 yards /60 metres per 100g)

US 6 (4mm) DPNs

US 8 (5mm) DPNs

US 8 (5mm) straight needles

US 11 (8mm) straight needles

Stitch holder

2¼ x 1in (5.5 x 2.5cm) black felt per eye and 2¼ x 1in (5.5 x 2.5cm) for the nose

¾in (21mm) black safety eyes x 2

Toy stuffing 1¼oz (35g) for the face and ¼oz (10g) for the ears

Wolf eye template (see Templates)

A small amount of chunky black yarn

Black cotton

DIMENSIONS

27 x 10¾in (70 x 27cm)

GAUGE (TENSION)

8.5 sts and 13 rows to 4in (10cm) over st st on US 11 (8mm) needles

16 sts and 23 rows to 4in (10cm) over st st on US 8 (5mm) needles

KNITTING TECHNIQUES

Long-tail cast on

Intarsia

Mattress stitch

Backstitch

HAT BASE

Using the long-tail CO method (see Techniques) and US 6 (4mm) DPNs, CO 84 sts in colour A. Join to work in the 1st round. This will make up the 1st round.

Round 2 *K1, p1* repeat from * to end.

Round 3 *K1, p1* repeat from * to end.

Round 4 Place 20 sts onto scrap yarn, k1, p1 across the remaining 64 sts.

Round 5 *K1, p1* all sts, knitting over the scrap yarn. (84 sts)

Repeat the 1 x 1 rib until the piece measures 1½in (4cm).

Change to US 8 (5mm) DPNs and work 15 rounds in st st.

Round 16 *K2tog, k10* repeat from * to end. (77 sts)

Round 17 K all sts.

Round 18 (dec) *K2tog, k9* repeat from * to end. (70 sts)

Round 19 K all sts.

Round 20 (dec) *K2tog, k8* repeat from * to end. (63 sts)

Round 21 K all sts.

Round 22 (dec) *K2tog, k7* repeat from * to end. (56 sts)

Round 23 K all sts.

Round 24 (dec) *K2tog, k6* repeat from * to end. (49 sts)

Round 25 K all sts.

Round 26 (dec) *K2tog, k5* repeat from * to end. (42 sts)

Round 27 K all sts.

Round 28 (dec) *K2tog, k4* repeat from * to end. (35 sts)

Round 29 K all sts.

Round 30 (dec) *K2tog, k3* repeat from * to end. (28 sts)

Round 31 K all sts.

Round 32 (dec) *K2tog, k2* repeat from * to end. (21 sts)

Round 33 K all sts.

Round 34 (dec) *K2tog, k1* repeat from * to end. (14 st)

Round 35 K all sts.

Round 36 (dec) K2tog to end. (7 sts)

Break yarn, leaving a long tail, thread through remaining live sts and pull through. Weave in ends.

TOP WOLF PIECE

Knitted separately to the bottom piece

Using the long-tail CO method (see Techniques) and US 8 (5mm) straight needles, CO 4 sts in colour C. This will make up the 1st row.

Row 2 P all st.

Row 3 (inc) *Kfb* repeat from * to end. (8 sts)

Row 4 P all sts.

Row 5 (inc) *Kfb, k1* repeat from * to end. (12 sts)

Row 6 P all sts.

Row 7 (inc) *Kfb, k2* repeat from * to end. (16 sts)

Row 8 P all sts.

Row 9 (inc) Kfb, k3, kfb, p1, k2, kfb, p1, k2, kfb, k3. (20 sts)

Row 10 P7, k1, p4, k1, p7.

Row 11 (inc) Kfb, k4, kfb, p2, k2, kfb, p2, k2, kfb, k4. (24 sts)

Row 12 P7, k2, p6, k2, p7.

Row 13 K6c, p3c, k2c, k2b, k2c, p3c, k6c.

Row 14 P6c, k3c, p1c, p4b, p1c, k3c, p6c.

Row 15 K5c, p3c, k1c, k6b, k1c, k3c, k5c.

Row 16 P5c, k3c, p1c, p6b, p1c, k3c, p5c.

Row 17 K4c, p4c, k8b, p4c, k4c.

Row 18 P4c, k4c, p8b, k4c, p4c.

Row 19 K3c, p4c, k10b, p4c, k3c.

Row 20 P3c, k4c, p10b, k4c, p3c.

Repeat the last 2 rows 2 times.

Row 25 (inc) Kfb in colour C, k2c, p4c, k10b, p4c, k2c, kfb in colour C. (26 sts)

Row 26 P4c, k4c, p10b, k4c, p4c.

Row 27 K4c, p4c, k10b, p4c, k4c.

Row 28 P4c, k4c, p10b, k4c, p4c.

Repeat the last 2 rows.

Row 31 K3c, p3c, k14b, p3c, k3c.

Row 32 P2c, k2c, p18b, k2c, p2c.

Row 33 K2c, k5b, p2b, k8b, p2b, k5b, k2c.

Row 34 Work all sts in colour B. P7, k2, p8, k2, p7.

Row 35 K8, p2, k6, p2, k8.

Row 36 P8, k2, p6, k2, p8.

Row 37 K9b, p2b, k1b, k2a, k1b, p2b, k9b.

Row 38 P9b, k2b, p4a, k2b, p9b.

Row 39 (inc) K2b [kfb, k1] x 4 in colour B, kfb in colour B, k1a, kfb in colour A, k1a, kfb in colour A, k1b, [kfb, k1] x 5 in colour B. (38 sts)

Row 40 P16b, p6a, p16b.

Row 41 (inc) K2b, [kfb, k2] x 4 in colour B, kfb in colour B, k2a, [kfb, k2] x 2 in colour A, [kfb, k2] x 5 in colour B. (50 sts)

Row 42 P20b, p10a, p20b.

Row 43 (inc) K2b, [kfb, k3] x 4 in colour B, kfb in colour B, k1b, k2a, [kfb, k3] x 2 in colour A, [kfb, k3] x 5 in colour B. (62 sts)

Row 44 P25b, p12a, p25b.

Row 45 (inc) K2b, [kfb, k4] x 4 in colour B, kfb in colour B, k1b, k3a, [kfb, k4] x 2 in colour A, [kfb, k4] x 5 in colour B. (74 sts)

Row 46 P29b, p16a, p29b.

Row 47 K27b, p2b, k16a, p2b, k27b.

Row 48 P27b, k2b, p16a, k2b, p27b.

Row 49 K26b, p2b, k18a, p2b, k26b.

Row 50 P26b, k2b, p18a, k2b, p26b.

Row 51 K25b, p2b, k20a, p2b, k25b.

Row 52 P25b, k2b, p20a, k2b, p25b.

Row 53 K24b, p2b, k22a, p2b, k24b.

Row 54 P24b, k2b, p22a, k2b, p24b.

Row 55 K20b, p5b, k24a, p5b, k20b.

Row 56 P20b, k5b, p24a, k5b, p20b.

Row 57 K17b, p5b, k30a, p5b, k17b.

Row 58 P17b, k5b, p30a, k5b, p17b.

Row 59 K15b, p4b, k36a, p4b, k15b.

Row 60 P15b, k4b, p36a, k4b, p15b.

Row 61 K13b, p3b, k42a, p3b, k13b.

Row 62 P13b, k3b, p42a, k3b, p13b.

Row 63 K11b, p2b, k48a, p2b, k11b.

Row 64 P11b, k2b, p48a, k2b, p11b.

Row 65 K9b, p1b, k54a, p1b, k9b.

Row 66 P9b, k1b, p54a, k1b, p9b.

Row 67 (inc) K2tog in colour B, k5b, k60a, k5b, k2tog in colour B. (72 sts)

Row 68 P3b, p66a, p3b.

Row 69 (dec) Work all sts in colour A, *k2tog, k6* repeat from * to end. (63 sts)

Row 70 P all sts.

Row 71 (dec) *K2tog, k5* repeat from * to end. (54 sts)

Row 72 P all sts.

Row 73 (dec) *K2tog, k4* repeat from * to end. (45 sts)

Row 74 P all sts.

Row 75 (dec) *K2tog, k3* repeat from * to end. (36 sts)

Row 76 P all sts.

Row 77 (dec) *K2tog, k2* repeat from * to end. (27 sts)

Row 78 P all sts.

Row 79 (dec) *K2tog, k1* repeat from * to end. (18 sts)

Row 80 P all sts.

Row 81 (dec) K2tog across all sts. (9 sts)

Row 82 P all sts.

Row 83 BO using US 11 (8mm) needles.

BOTTOM OF SNOUT

Cut the scrap yarn holding the 20 stitches then pick up both sides. It may be easier to use a US 6 (4mm) DPN.

Take 1 st from the front needle and place on the back. Using colour A purl both together and repeat for all sts using a US 8 (5mm) straight needle. Make sure the decreased part of the hat is facing towards you when doing this. Repeat this for all sts. (20 sts)

Row 1 (inc) *Kfb, k4* repeat from * to end. (24 sts)

Row 2 P1b, p22a, p1b.

Row 3 K2b, k20a, k2b.

Row 4 P3b, p18a, p3b.

Row 5 K4b, k16a, k4b.

Row 6 P1c, p5b, p12a, p5b, p1c.

Row 7 K2c, k6b, k8a, k6b, k2c.

Row 8 P3c, p7b, p4a, p7b, p3c.

Row 9 K4c, k16b, k4c.

Row 10 P5c, k14b, p5c.

Row 11 (dec) K2tog in colour C, k4c, k2tog in colour B, k4b, k2tog in colour B, k4b, k2tog in colour C, k4c. (20 sts)

Row 12 P6c, p8b, p6c.

Row 13 (dec) K2tog in colour C, k3c, k2tog in colour C, k1c, k2b, k2tog in colour B, k1b, k2c, k2tog in colour C, k3c. (16 sts)

Row 14 P7c, p2b, p7c.

Row 15 (dec) *K2tog, k2* repeat from * to end in colour C. (12 sts)

Row 16 P all sts.

Row 17 (dec) *K2tog, k1* repeat from * to end. (8 sts)

Row 18 P all sts.

Row 19 (dec) K2tog across all sts. (4 sts)

BO

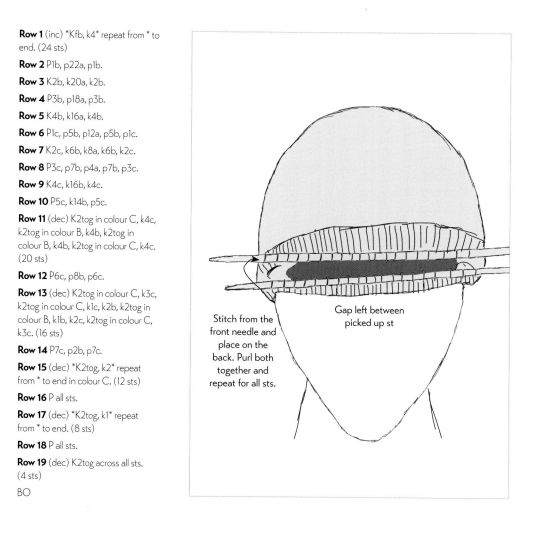

Stitch from the front needle and place on the back. Purl both together and repeat for all sts.

Gap left between picked up st

BOUCLÉ FALLS

Pick up 17 sts evenly across the BO edge of the Top Wolf Piece. If it is easier, you could use the US 6 (4mm) needle, ready to k the sts using colour D and US 10 (7mm) needles.

Row 1 K all sts.

Row 2 (inc) Kfbf, k15, kfbf. (21 sts)

Row 3 (inc) Kfbf, k19, kfbf. (25 sts)

Row 4 (inc) Kfbf, k23, kfbf. (29 sts)

Row 5 (inc) Kfbf, k27, kfbf.(33 sts)

Row 6 (inc) Kfbf, k31, kfbf. (37 sts)

Row 7 (inc) Kfbf, k35, kfbf. (41 sts)

Row 8 (inc) Kfbf, k39, kfbf. (45 sts)

Work in garter st until the piece measures 6½in (17cm).

Row 1 K22, leave the remaining 23 sts on a stitch holder.

Row 2 (dec) K2tog, k to end. (21 sts)

Row 4 (dec) K2tog, k to end. (20 sts)

Row 5 K all sts.

Repeat rows 4 and 5, 7 times until there are 13 sts remaining.

Work in garter st until the piece measures 16in (40cm) and BO.

Place the unworked 23 sts back on the needle.

Row 1 (dec) K2tog, k to end. (22 sts)

Row 2 K all sts.

Row 3 (dec) K2tog, k to end. (21 sts)

Row 4 K all sts.

Repeat rows 4 and 5 (above), 8 more times until there are 13 sts remaining.

Work in garter st until the piece measures 8in (40cm) and BO.

FRONT EARS

Make 2

Using the long-tail CO method and US 8 (5mm) straight needles, CO 18 sts in colour A. This will make up the 1st row.

Row 2 P all st.

Row 3 K8a, k2c, k8a.

Row 4 P7a, p4a, p7a.

Row 5 K6a, k6c, k6a.

Row 6 P5a, p8c, p5a.

Row 7 (dec) K2tog in colour A, k2a, k2c, k2tog in colour C, k4c, k2tog in colour C, k1c, k3a. (15 sts)

Row 8 P3a, p9c, p3a.

Row 9 K3a, k9c, k3a.

Row 10 P3a, p9c, p3a.

Row 11 K3a, k9c, k3a.

Row 12 P3a, p9c, p3a.

Row 13 (dec) K2tog in colour A, k2a, k1c, k2tog in colour C, k3c, k2tog in colour C, k3a. (12 sts)

Row 14 P3a, p6c, p3a.

Row 15 K3a, k6c, k3a.

Row 16 P3a, p6c, p3a.

Row 17 (dec) K2tog in colour A, k2a, k2tog in colour C, k2c, k2tog in colour A, k2. (9 sts)

Row 18 P3a, p3c, p3a.

Row 19 (dec) Work all sts in colour A. *K2tog, k1* repeat from * to end. (6 sts)

Row 20 P all sts.

Row 21 (dec) K2tog to end. (3 sts)

Break yarn, leaving a long tail, thread through remaining live sts and pull through. Weave in ends.

BACK EARS

Make 2

Using the long-tail CO method and US 8 (5mm) straight needles, CO 18 sts in colour A. This will make up the 1st row.

Row 2 P all sts.

Work 4 rows in st st.

Row 7 (dec) *K2tog, k4* repeat from * to end. (15 sts)

Work 5 rows in st st.

Row 13 (dec) *K2tog, k3* repeat from * to end. (12 sts)

Work 3 rows in st st.

Row 17 (dec) *K2tog, k2* repeat from * to end. (9 sts)

Row 18 P all sts.

Row 19 (dec) *K2tog, k1* repeat from * to end. (6 sts)

Row 20 P all sts.

Row 21 (dec) K2tog across all sts. (3 sts)

Break yarn, leaving a long tail, thread through remaining live sts and pull through. Weave in ends.

MAKING UP

Take the two nose pieces, the Hat Base and Top Wolf Piece, and place them so the insides are facing. Pin from either side of the point where the peak was made (from the scrap yarn).

Sew up using corresponding yarn colours. Turn inside out and stuff the newly made nose. The top piece of the wolf will now sit over the Hat Base and the Bouclé Falls will cover the area that the Top Wolf Piece does not. Sew the BO edge of the Top Wolf Piece onto the Hat Base neatly in colour A.

Pin both sides of the Bouclé Falls so they sit on top of the Hat Base but will be covered by the wolf's cheeks, following the natural line of the garter st. The Bouclé Falls will sit most of the way round the hat. Leaving a gap of 5in (13cm) between it and the nose. Sew the Bouclé Falls neatly into the hat using colour A and backstitch (see Techniques).

Then place the 1¼oz (35g) of stuffing evenly into the wolf's head. Cut two of the eyepieces and one nose from the felt. Fold the eyes in half and cut a very small slit in the centre. This will allow for the toy safety eyes to be pushed through. Then place both eyes onto the head, 3¼in (8.5cm) from the start of the light grey, (4½in [12cm] from the CO edge) with the bottom point ¼ in (0.5cm) from the edge of the dark grey on the face and the top of it 1in (2.5cm) from the edge. Secure the eyes in place. You can add a few stitches in cotton thread or fabric glue to secure. Then pin the nose just under the start of the light grey in the centre. Using a small amount of chunky black yarn, sew a few spots either side of the face.

Take one front ear and one back ear and place them together. Sew up using mattress st (see Techniques) in colour A. Stuff using ⅛oz (5g) per ear. Place the ears 10in (25cm) from the CO sts, sitting on the edge of the dark grey colour and 3¼ in (8.5cm) from the side of the cheek.

Then sew the bottom of the cheeks into the Bouclé Falls, following the snout and sewing up in the corresponding colours using a very neat backstitch.

THE PLAITS

Cut 54 strands of bouclé, measuring 12in (30cm) each. Then take three pieces, tie a knot at the top and plait. Tie at the bottom, leaving a small amount of the three yarns un-plaited. Sew nine plaits each side of the bottom of the bouclé, using a large sewing needle and the bouclé yarn, leaving an equal gap between them.

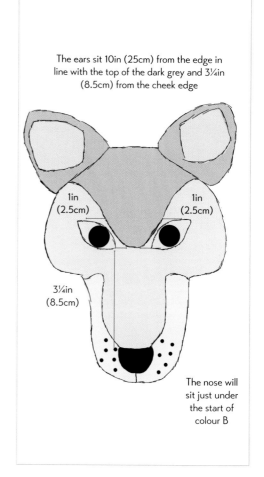

The ears sit 10in (25cm) from the edge in line with the top of the dark grey and 3¼in (8.5cm) from the cheek edge

1in (2.5cm)

1in (2.5cm)

3¼in (8.5cm)

The nose will sit just under the start of colour B

DON'T FORGET THE PLAITS, THEY ADD A GREAT FINISH TO THE BOUCLÉ. TRY SEWING IN A FEW FEATHERS AND BEADS TO MAKE IT MORE AUTHENTIC.

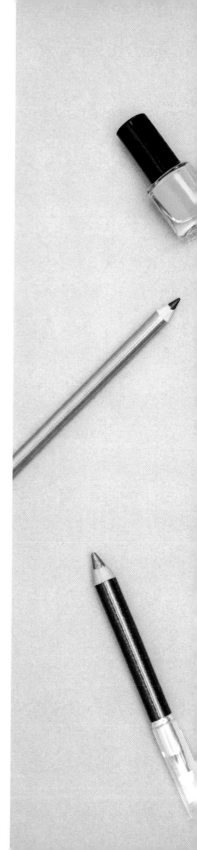

CROCODILE MAKE-UP BAG

SKILL LEVEL
INTERMEDIATE

Mock croc rocks! This mock-croc design is not only more

ethical, but also you never need worry about where to

keep your mascara again.

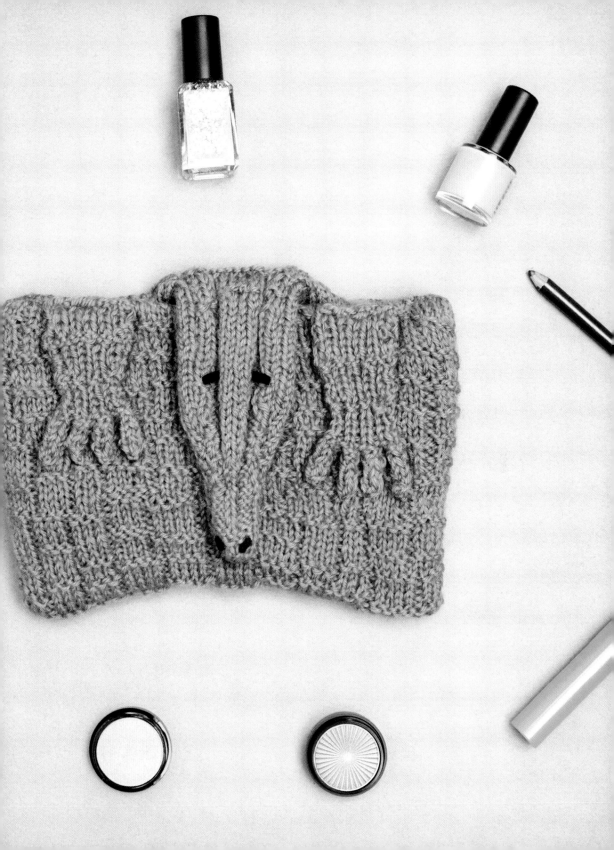

MATERIALS

Sincerely Louise, Swamp x 1 ball (246 yards/225m per 100g)

US 6 (4mm) straight needles

Stitch holder

12 x 18in (30 x 46cm) black lining

Black cotton

Fabric glue

1 popper

2 x 1¼ x ½in (3 x 1cm) black felt for the eyes

2 x ½ x ½in (1 x 1cm) black felt for the nostrils

Crocodile eyes and nose template (see Templates)

DIMENSIONS

8¼ x 5 ½in (21 x 14cm)

GAUGE (TENSION)

22 sts and 30 rows to 4in (10cm) over st st

KNITTING TECHNIQUES

Long-tail cast on

Mattress stitch

Backstitch

MAIN BAG

Using the long-tail CO method (see Techniques) and US 6 (4mm) needles, CO 57 sts.

Begin working from the chart. The blank squares represent the knit st and circles the purl st.

Work the chart, ending at row 90.

Row 91 BO 18 sts, k2, p1, k4, p1, k4, p1, k4, p1, k3, p1, k4, p1, k3, p1, k4, p4. (39 sts)

Row 92 BO 18 sts purlwise, p3, k1, p4, k1, p4, k1, p4, k1, p2. (21 sts)

Row 93 K2, p1, k4, p1, k4, p9.

Row 94 P3, k1, p4, k13.

Row 95 (dec) Ssk, k1, p1, k3, p1, k4, p1, k4, p1, k1, k2tog. (19 sts)

Row 96 P2, k1, p4, k1, p4, k1, p3, k1, p2.

Row 97 (dec) Ssk, p1, k3, p1, k4 p1, k4, p1, k2tog. (17 sts)

Row 98 K all sts.

Row 99 K1, p1, k2, p2, k5, p2, k2, p1, k1.

Row 100 P1, k1, p2, k2, p5, k2, p2, k1, p1.

Row 101 K1, p1, k2, p2, k5, p2, k2, p2.

Row 102 P1, k1, p2, k2, p5, k6.

Row 103 P2, k3, p2, k5, p5, k1.

Row 104 P1, k1, p2, k2, p5, k2, p2, k2.

Row 105 P2, k2, p2, k5, p2, k2, p1, k1.

Row 106 K6, p5, k6.

Row 107 K3, p3, k5, p3, k3.

Row 108 P3, k3, p5, k3, p3.

Row 109 K3, p3, k5, p3, k3.

Row 110 P3, k3, p5, k3, p3.

Row 111 K3, p3, k5, p3, k3.

Row 112 P3, k3, p5, k3, p3.

Row 113 K3, p3, k5, p3, k3.

Row 114 K6, p5, p6.

Row 115 K3, p3, k5, p3, k3.

Row 116 P3, k3, p5, k3, p3.

Row 117 K3, p3, k5, p3, k3.

Row 118 P3, k4, p3, k4, p3.

Row 119 (dec) Ssk, k1, p4, k4, p4, k1, k2tog. (15 sts)

Row 120 P3, k3, p3, k3, p3.

Row 121 (dec) Ssk, k1, p3, k3, p3, k1, k2tog. (13 sts)

Row 122 P3, k2, p3, k2, p3.

Row 123 (dec) Ssk, k1, p2, k3, p2, k1, k2tog. (11 sts)

Row 124 P3, k2, p1, k2, p3.

Row 125 (dec) Ssk, k1, p2, k1, p2, k1, k2tog. (9 sts)

Row 126 P2, k2, p1, k2, p2.

Row 127 K2, p2, k1, p2, k2.

Row 128 P2, k2, p1, k2, p2.

Row 129 K2, p2, k1, p2, k2.

Row 130 P2, k2, p1, k2, p2.

Row 131 K2, p2, k1, p2, k2.

Row 132 P2, k5, p2.

Row 133 K3, k3, p3.

Row 134 P all sts.

Row 135 (dec) *K2tog, k1* repeat from * to end. (6 sts)

Row 136 P all sts.

Row 137 (dec) *K2tog* repeat from * to end. (3sts)

Row 138 P all sts.

Row 139 (inc) *Kfb* repeat from * to end. (6 sts)

Row 140 P all sts.

Row 141 (inc) *Kfb, k1* repeat from * to end. (9 sts)

Work 9 rows in st st.

Row 151 (inc) Kfb, k7, kfb. (11 sts)

Row 153 (inc) Kfb, k9 kfb. (13 sts)

Row 154 P all sts.

Row 155 (inc) Kfb, k11, kfb. (15 sts)

Row 156 P all sts.

Row 157 (inc) Kfb, k13, kfb. (17 sts)

Work 21 rows in st st.

Row 179 (inc) Kfb, k15, kfb. (19 sts)

Row 181 (inc) Kfb, k17, kfb. (21 sts)

Row 183 K all sts.

Row 184 CO 18 sts purlwise. (39 sts)

Row 185 CO 18 sts. (57 sts)

Row 187 K all sts.

Row 189 K all sts.

Row 191 K all sts.

BO

LEGS

Make 2

Using the long-tail CO method (see Techniques) and US 6 (4mm) straight needles, CO 12 sts. This will make up the 1st row.

Row 2 P all sts.

Row 3 *K1, p1* repeat from * to end.

Repeat row 3, 4 more times.

Row 8 (dec) K2tog, k8, k2tog. (10 sts)

Row 9 *K1, p1* repeat from * to end.

Repeat row 9, 4 more times.

Row 14 (dec) K2tog, k6, k2tog. (8 sts)

Row 15 *K1, p1* repeat from * to end.

Repeat row 15, 14 more times.

Row 30 (inc) *Kfb, k1* repeat from * to end. (12 sts)

Row 31 K3 and turn, leave the other 9 sts on a stitch holder.

Row 32 P all sts.

Row 33 K all sts.

Row 34 P all sts.

Row 35 K all sts.

Row 36 (dec) P3tog.

Break yarn, leaving a long tail, thread through remaining live sts and pull through. Weave in ends.

CLAWS

Pick up the 9 sts placed on a stitch holder at row 21.

Repeat rows 21–24, four more times, picking up 9 sts the first time, 6 sts the second time and 3 the third time. This will create the claws.

MARK THE PATTERN OFF IN PENCIL AS YOU GO ALONG TO MAKE SURE YOU DON'T MAKE ANY MISTAKES.

MAKING UP

Block your crocodile. Weave in the ends. Lay the bag flat and, using the black lining, cut a rectangle matching the crocodile's body. Leave the two face pieces unlined. Pin the lining to the WS of the piece and sew up in black cotton.

Fold the lined body in half with the RS of the piece facing in. Sew the sides up. Fold the head onto itself (with the WS facing in) pin and sew up using mattress st (see Techniques). Then pin the extra CO edges onto the lining of the bag. Pin and sew along the BO edge into the lining using a careful backstitch (see Techniques) and black cotton. Add a few sts on the top corners of the bag (this will make it more secure).

Turn the bag so the RS is facing out, and the lining facing in. Place the popper so the centre sits 1⅜in (3½cm) from the bottom of the bag and crocodile face, sitting in the centre. Sew up using colour A. The face of the bag will now fit nicely over the gap and onto the popper.

Place the legs on to the front of the bag leaving a ¾in (2cm) gap from the edge. Cut two eyes and two nostrils in black felt from the templates (see Templates). Place the eyes 3¼in (8cm) from the bottom of the face, leaving a ½in (1cm) gap. They should sit nicely over the purl indents and point slightly upwards towards, each other. The nostrils should sit at the bottom of the nose, pointing up and away from each other. Sew up using black cotton.

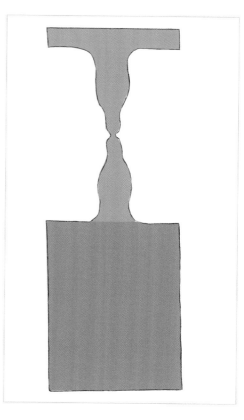

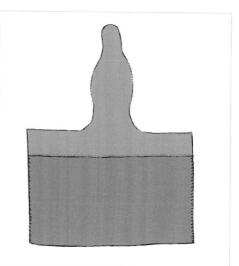

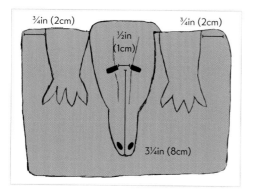

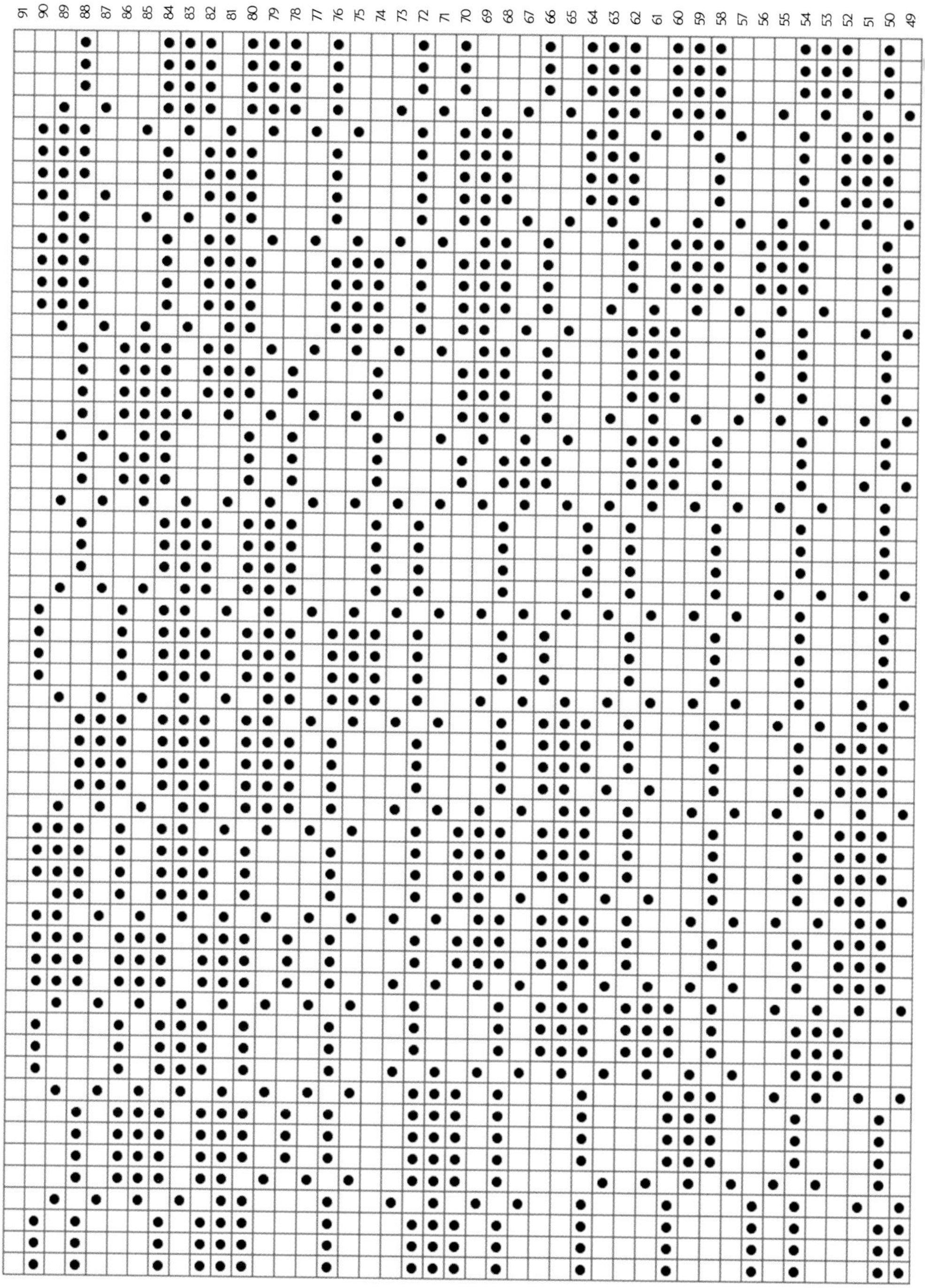

CHART
KEY

Knit ☐

Purl ☑

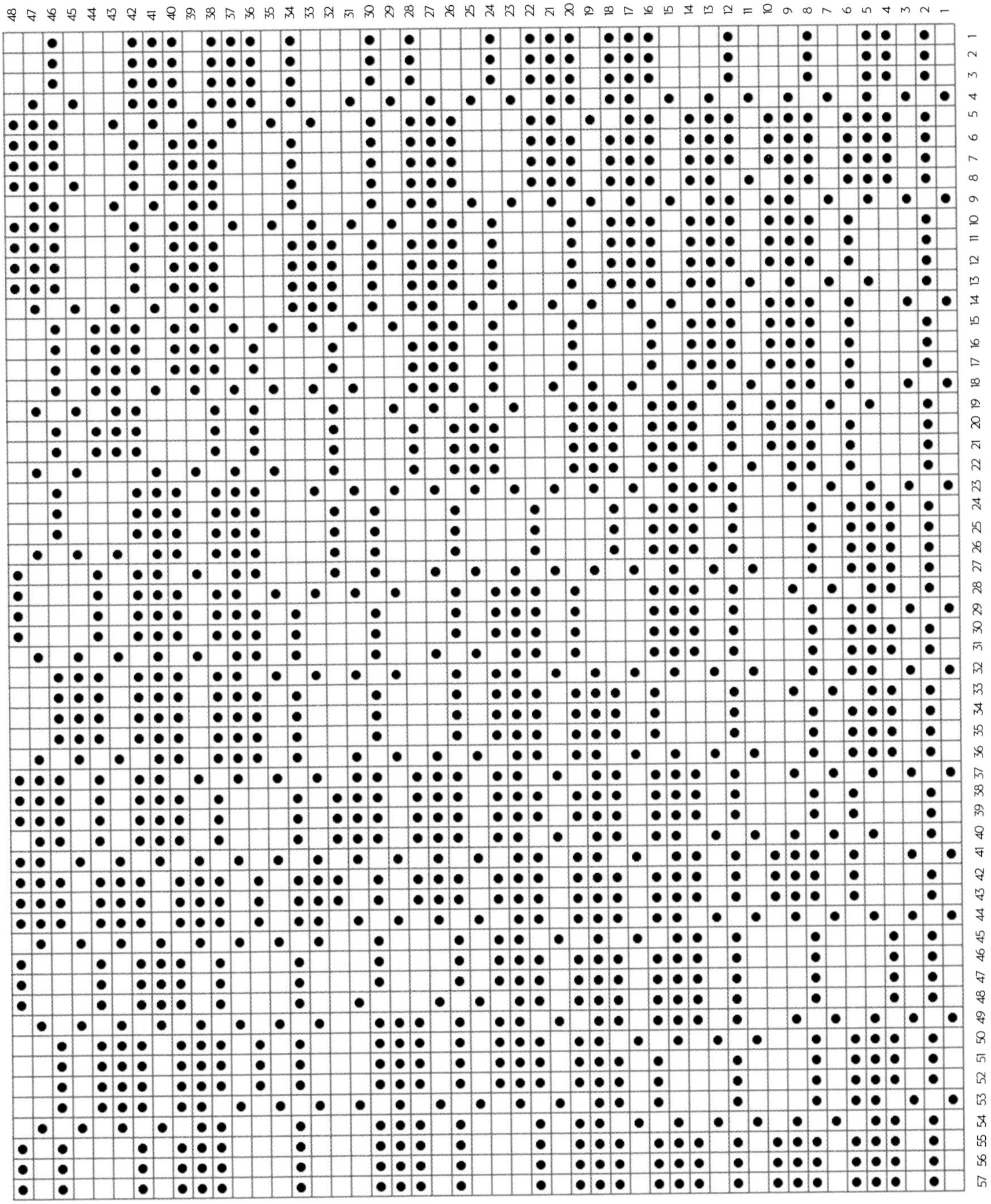

HABITAT

MOOSE HEAD

SKILL LEVEL
INTERMEDIATE

This cheeky chap has to be the epitome of all faux

taxidermy knits. He's comical, charismatic and, if you

look really closely, you might spot a wry smile amongst

the knits and purls!

MATERIALS

A Sincerely Louise Aran Bluefaced Leicester, Moose x 2 balls (246 yards/225 metres per 100g)

B Sincerely Louise Aran Bluefaced Leicester, Mustard x 1 balls (246 yards/225 metres per 100g)

US 7 (4.5mm) needles

2 x 1¼in (30mm) black safety eyes

1½ x 2½in (4 x 6cm) black felt per nostril

Black sewing thread or fabric glue

Moose and Moose nostril templates (see Templates)

⅟₁₆in (2mm) cardboard

46in (116cm) piece of flower wire x 2

9oz (250g) stuffing

DIMENSIONS

26 x 12 x 11in (67 x 30 x 28cm)

GAUGE (TENSION)

19 sts and 24 rows to 4in (10cm) over st st

KNITTING TECHNIQUES

Long-tail cast on

Mattress stitch

TOP PIECE

Using the long-tail CO method (see Techniques) and US 7 (4.5mm) needles, CO 4 sts in colour A. This will make up the 1st row.

Row 2 P all sts.

Row 3 (inc) Kfb to end. (8 sts)

Row 4 P all sts.

Row 5 (inc) Kfb to end. (16 sts)

Row 6 P all sts.

Row 7 (inc) *Kfb, k1* repeat from * to end. (24 sts)

Row 8 P all sts.

Row 9 (inc) *Kfb, k2* repeat from * to end. (32 sts)

Row 10 P all sts.

Row 11 (inc)*Kfb, k3* repeat from * to end. (40 sts)

Row 12 P all sts.

Row 13 (inc) *Kfb, k4* repeat from * to end. (48 sts)

Row 14 P all sts.

Row 15 (inc) *Kfb, k5* repeat from * to end. (56 sts)

Work the next 35 rows in st st.

Row 51 (inc) Kfb, k54, kfb. (58 sts)

Row 52 P all sts.

Row 53 (inc) K1, kfb, k54, kfb, k1. (60 sts)

Row 54 P all sts.

Row 55 (inc) K2, kfb, k54, kfb, k2. (62 sts)

Row 56 P all sts.

Row 57 (inc) K3, kfb, k54, kfb, k3. (64 sts)

Row 58 P all sts.

Row 59 (inc) K4, kfb, k54, kfb, k4. (66 sts)

Row 60 P all sts.

Row 61 (inc) K5, kfb, k54, kfb, k5. (68 sts)

Row 62 P all sts.

Row 63 (inc) K6, kfb, k54, kfb, k6. (70 sts)

Row 64 P all sts.

Row 65 (dec) K7, kfb, [k2tog, k1] x 18, kfb, k7. (54 sts)

Row 66 P all sts.

Row 67 (inc) K8, kfb, k36, kfb, k8. (56 sts)

Row 68 P all sts.

Row 69 (inc) K9, kfb, [kfb, k5] x 6, kfb, k9. (64 sts)

Row 70 P all sts.

Row 71 (inc) K10, kfb, k42, kfb, k10. (66 sts)

Row 72 P all sts.

Row 73 (inc) K11, kfb, [kfb, k6] x 6, kfb, k11. (74 sts)

Row 74 P all sts.

Row 75 (inc) K12, kfb, k48, kfb, k12. (76 sts)

Row 76 P all sts.

Row 77 (inc) K13, kfb, [kfb, k7] x 6, kfb, k13. (84 sts)

Row 78 P all sts.

Row 79 (inc) K14, kfb, k54, kfb, k14. (86 sts)

Row 80 P all sts.

Row 81 (inc) K15, kfb, k54, kfb, k15. (88 sts)

Row 82 P all sts.

Row 83 (inc) K16, kfb, k54, kfb, k16. (90 sts)

Row 84 P all sts.

Row 85 (inc) K17, kfb, k54, kfb, k17. (92 sts)

Row 86 P all sts.

Row 87 (inc) K18, kfb, k54, kfb, k18. (94 sts)

Work the next 15 rows in st st.

Row 103 (dec) K18, k2tog, k54, k2tog, k18. (92 sts)

Row 104 P all sts.

Row 105 (dec) *K2tog, k2* repeat from * to end. (69 sts)

Work the next 3 rows in st st.

Row 109 (dec) *K2tog, k1* repeat from * to end. (46 sts)

Row 110 P all sts.

Row 111 K all sts.

Row 112 P all sts.

Row 113 (dec) *K2tog* to end. (23 sts)

Row 114 P all sts.

Row 115 (dec) [K2tog] x 11, k1. (12 sts)

Row 116 P all sts.

BO

UNDER PIECE

Work the pattern for Top Piece until row 50.

Work 12 rows in st st.

Row 63 (inc) *Kfb, k6* repeat from * to end. (64 sts)

Work 3 rows in st st.

Row 67 (inc) *Kfb, k7* repeat from * to end. (72 sts)

Work 3 rows in st st.

Row 71 (inc) *Kfb, k8* repeat from * to end. (80 sts)

Work 3 rows in st st.

Row 75 (inc) *Kfb, k9* repeat from * to end. (88 sts)

Work 5 rows in st st.

Row 81 (inc) *Kfb, k10* repeat from * to end. (96 sts)

Row 82 P all sts.

Work 8 rows in st st.

BO

ANTLERS

Make two of both antler patterns, they are a mirror image of each other, so one of each make up the fronts and one of each make up the backs.

Make 2 (1 x front and 1 x back)

Using the long-tail CO method (see Techniques) and US 7 (4.5mm) needles, CO 10 sts in colour B. This will make up the 1st row.

Row 2 P all sts.

Row 3 K all sts.

Row 4 P all sts.

Work the next 12 rows in st st.

Row 15 (inc) K8, kfb, k1. (11 sts)

Work the next 5 rows in st st.

Row 21 (inc) K9, kfb, k1. (12 sts)

Row 22 P all sts.

Row 23 (inc) K10, kfb, k1. (13 sts)

Row 24 CO 4, and p all sts. (17 sts)

Row 25 (inc) K1, kfb, k13, kfb, k1. (19 sts)

Row 26 CO 2 sts and p all sts. (21 sts)

Work the next 6 rows in st st.

Row 33 (dec) K18, k2tog, k1. (20 sts)

Row 34 BO 4 sts purlwise, and p all sts. (16 sts)

Row 35 (dec) K13, k2tog, k1. (15 sts)

Work 3 rows in st st.

Row 39 (inc) K13, kfb, k1. (16 sts)

Row 40 P all sts.

Row 41 (inc) K14, kfb, k1. (17 sts)

Row 42 CO 2 sts and p all sts. (19 sts)

Row 43 (inc) K17, kfb, k1. (20 sts)

Row 44 P all sts.

Row 45 (inc) K18, kfb, k1. (21 sts)

Row 46 CO 2 sts and p all sts. (23 sts)

Row 47 (inc) K21, kfb, k1. (24 sts)

Row 48 P all sts.

Row 49 (inc) K22, kfb, k1. (25 sts)

Row 50 P all sts.

Row 51 (dec) K22, k2tog, k1. (24sts)

Row 52 P all sts.

Row 53 (dec) K21, k2tog, k1. (23 sts)

Row 54 BO 4 sts purlwise. (19 sts)

Row 55 (dec) K16, k2tog, k1. (18 sts)

Row 56 BO 2 sts purlwise. (16 sts)

Row 57 (inc) K14, kfb k1. (17 sts)

Row 58 P all sts.

Row 59 (inc) K15, kfb, k1. (18 sts)

Row 60 CO 2 sts and p all sts. (20 sts)

Row 61 (inc) K18, kfb, k1. (21 sts)

Row 62 CO 2 sts and p all sts. (23 sts)

Row 63 (inc) K21, kfb, k1. (24 sts)

Row 64 CO 2 sts and p all sts. (26 sts)

Row 65 (inc) K24, kfb, k1. (27 sts)

Work 7 rows in st st.

Row 73 (dec) K1, k2tog, k24. (26 sts)

Row 74 P all sts.

Row 75 (dec) BO 2 sts, k21, k2tog, k1. (23 sts)

Row 76 P all sts.

Row 77 (dec) BO 2 sts, k18, k2tog, k1. (20 sts)

Row 78 P all sts.

Row 79 (dec) BO 2 sts, k15, k2tog, k1. (17 sts)

Row 80 BO 3 sts purlwise. (14 sts)

BO

Reverse Antler

Make 2 (1 x front, 1 x back)

Row 1 CO 10 sts using long-tail CO method.

Row 2 P all sts.

Work 12 rows in st st.

Row 15 (inc) K1, kfb, k8. (11 sts)

Work 5 rows in st st.

Row 21 (inc) K1, kfb, k9. (12 sts)

Row 22 P all sts.

Row 23 (inc) CO 5 sts and k all sts. (17 sts)

Row 24 P all sts.

Row 25 (inc) K1, kfb, k13, kfb, k1. (19 sts)

Row 26 P all sts.

Row 27 CO 2 sts and k all sts. (21 sts)

Work 5 rows in st st.

Row 33 (dec) K1, k2tog, k18. (20 sts)

Row 34 P all sts.

Row 35 BO 4 sts. (16 sts)

Row 36 (dec) P1, p2tog, p13. (15 sts)

Row 37 K all sts.

Row 38 P all sts.

Row 39 (inc) K1, kfb, k13. (16 sts)

Row 40 P all sts.

Row 41 (inc) K1, kfb, k14. (17 sts)

Row 42 P all sts.

Row 43 CO 3 sts and k all sts. (20 sts)

Row 44 P all sts.

Row 45 (inc) K1, kfb, k18. (21 sts)

Row 46 P all sts.

Row 47 CO 3 sts and k to end. (24 sts)

Row 48 P all sts.

Row 49 (inc) K1, kfb, k22. (25 sts)

Row 50 P all sts.

Row 51 (dec) K1, k2tog, k22. (24 sts)

Row 52 P all sts.

Row 53 (dec) K1, k2tog, k21. (23 sts)

Row 54 (dec) P1, p2tog, p20. (22 sts)

Row 55 BO 5 sts and k to end. (17 sts)

Row 56 (dec) P1, p2tog, p14. (16 sts)

Row 57 (inc) K1, kfb, k14. (17 sts)

Row 58 P all sts.

Row 59 CO 3 sts and k to end. (20 sts)

Row 60 P all sts.

Row 61 CO 3 sts and k to end. (23 sts)

Row 62 P all sts.

Row 63 CO 3 sts and k to end. (26 sts)

Row 64 P all sts.

Row 65 (inc) K1, kfb, k24. (27 sts)

Work 5 rows in st st.

Row 71 (dec) K24, k2tog, k1. (26 sts)

Row 72 P all sts.

Row 73 (dec) K1, k2tog, k23. (25 sts)

Row 74 BO 2 sts purlwise and p all. (23 sts)

Row 75 (dec) K1, k2tog, k20. (22 sts)

Row 76 BO 2 sts purlwise and p all. (20 sts)

Row 77 (dec) K1, k2tog, k17. (19 sts)

Row 78 BO 2 sts purlwise and p all. (17 sts)

Row 79 (dec) K1, k2tog, k14. (16 sts)

Row 80 BO 2 sts purlwise and p all. (14 sts)

BO

EARS

Make 4

Using the long-tail CO method (see Techniques) and US 7 (4.5mm) needles, CO 14 st in colour A. This will make up the 1st row.

Work 3 rows in st st.

Row 5 (inc) K1, kfb, k10, kfb, k1. (16 sts)

Work 3 rows in st st.

Row 9 (inc) K1, kfb, k12, kfb, k1. (18 sts)

Work 5 rows in st st.

Row 15 (dec) K1, k2tog, k12, k2tog, k1. (16 sts)

Row 16 P all sts.

Row 17 (dec) K1, k2tog, k10, k2tog, k1. (14 sts)

Row 18 P all sts.

Row 19 (dec) K1, k2tog, k8, k2tog, k1. (12 sts)

Row 20 P all sts.

Row 21 (dec) K1, k2tog, k6, k2tog, k1. (10 sts)

Row 22 P all sts.

Row 23 (dec) K1, k2tog, k4, k2tog, k1. (8 sts)

Row 24 P all sts.

Row 25 (dec) K1, k2tog, k2, k2tog, k1. (6 sts)

Row 26 P all sts.

Row 27 K1, [k2tog] x 2, k1. (4 sts)

Row 28 P all sts.

BO

MAKING UP

Pin and sew up the two ear pieces using mattress st (see Techniques). Stuff lightly.

Sew the top piece of the moose to the bottom using mattress st (the bottom is shorter than the top to help with the shaping). Cut two nostrils out of black felt and place them 1¼in (3cm) from the CO edge, leaving a 1½ (4cm) gap between them in the centre. Sew up using black cotton or use strong fabric glue. Then place the two eyes on the line made by the increases, leaving 2¾ in (7cm) between them in the centre and 5½ in (14cm) from the open edge. Place the ears ¾in (2cm) from the open edge and 8½in (22cm) from the bottom of the moose head. Sew up using colour A.

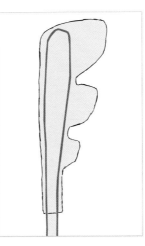

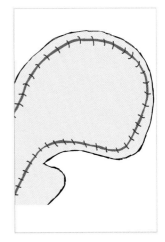

ANTLERS

Make 2

Take the flower wire and fold it in half. Lay ½in (1cm) on the edge of the WS of the knitted antler (leaving out the shaped sides) then over the wire and sew into place. Place the second antler over the first and use colour B and mattress stitch to sew up. Then add the stuffing (you may need a knitting needle to push it into shape).

Half stuff the moose head (forming its shape but leaving the top part empty). Then place the antlers 1½in (4cm) from the back edge, with 5in (13cm) between them in the centre. They will be ¾in (2cm) away from the ears. When placing the antlers on to the head of the moose push the extra wire though the head. Then, on the inside of the moose, take the wire and fold, then sew up using colour A.

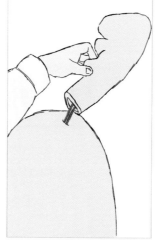

MOUNTING

Cut two templates (see Templates) and place over ¹⁄₁₆in (2mm) thick cardboard. Draw around and cut out. With the template still over the cardboard, place pins into the marked holes.

Remove the pins and, using a big sewing needle, push into and through the holes. Place the back of the Moose Head against the cardboard with the BO edges ⅝in (1.5cm) over it. Pin the edges and sides all the way around at intervals, avoiding the holes made earlier.

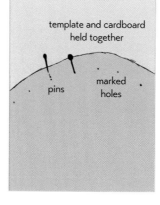

template and cardboard held together

pins

marked holes

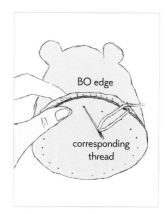

BO edge

corresponding thread

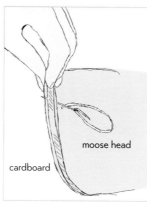

cardboard

moose head

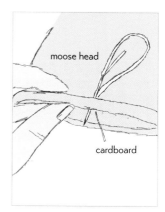

moose head

cardboard

Take a corresponding colour thread and sew into the top hole. Push through into the back of the head, pull the yarn but leave a tail. Sew the yarn back into the head. Pull through and sew into the next hole.

Repeat this process anticlockwise around the head, but leave a gap on the last quarter.

Now add the second template over the first, covering all the sewing. Repeat the template sewing up process again sewing through the holes made in the first template. You don't need to leave a gap this time. This will secure your moose safely in place.

Use a small amount of flower wire and sew through the top hole, make a loop and tie with a strong knot. Sew the ends back into the piece. Weave in loose ends.

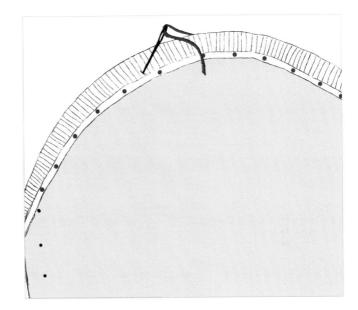

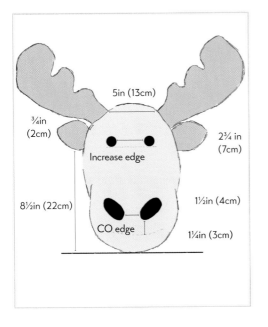

5in (13cm)

¾in (2cm)

2¾ in (7cm)

Increase edge

8½in (22cm)

1½in (4cm)

CO edge

1¼in (3cm)

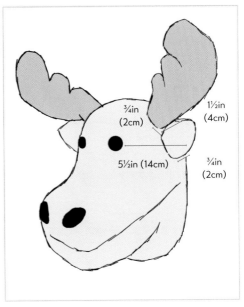

¾in (2cm)

1½in (4cm)

5½in (14cm)

¾in (2cm)

FINISHING THE ANTLERS

Using colour B sew into the bottom of the antlers, then take your needle and sew it ¾in (2cm) into the antlers. Then sew directly below it and into the moose. Leave a good gap and push the needle out. Then sew directly above it, ¾in (2cm) into the antler, pushing the needle out approximately where you started, pull tight and repeat this process around the antler. This will sew it securely into place.

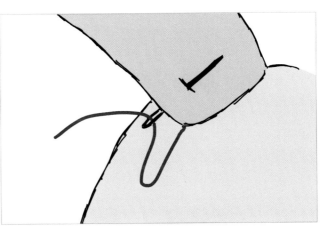

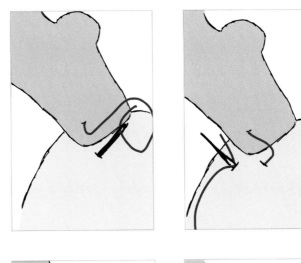

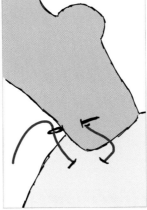

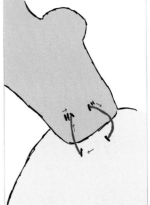

DON'T WORRY IF YOUR MOOSE FEELS A LITTLE SLACK, ONCE HE'S STUFFED AND SEWN ONTO THE TEMPLATE HE'LL LOOK GREAT ABOVE THE FIREPLACE.

OWL COSY

SKILL LEVEL
INTERMEDIATE

Eccentric, delightful and quirky – every teapot needs an

Owl Cosy, so why not treat yours to a beautifully crafted

homemade one? While you're at it, you could bake up a

batch of cookies to go with the tea if you like!

MATERIALS

A Brooklyn Tweed, Shelter, Nest x 2 balls (140 yards/128 metres per 50g)

B Brooklyn Tweed, Shelter, Pumpernickel x 1 ball (140 yards/128 metres per 50g)

C Brooklyn Tweed, Shelter, Snowbound x 1 ball (140 yards/128 metres per 50g)

D Robin, Double Knit, Apple x 1 ball (328 yards/300 metres per 100g)

US 7 (4.5mm) straight needles

US 7 (4.5mm) DPNs

US 6 (4mm) straight needles

Stitch holder

Mustard felt

Grey felt

Black felt

Very small amount of cream DK yarn

Owl templates (see Templates)

⅛oz (4.5g) of stuffing per owl

Black, white and mustard cottons or strong fabric glue

DIMENSIONS

8 x 8 x 8½in (20 x 20 x 22cm)

GAUGE (TENSION)

20 sts and 28 rows to 4in (10cm) over st st using worsted weight wool and US 7 (4.5mm) needles

24 sts and 32 rows to 4in (10cm) over st st using DK weight wool and US 6 (4mm) needles

KNITTING TECHNIQUES

Long-tail cast on

SIZE

All tea cosies vary in size. This pattern is suited to a four-cup teapot but can easily be adapted to fit other sizes of teapot. If needed, add extra rows of garter stitch at the start of the sides.

TEA COSY BASE

Make 2

Using the long-tail CO method (see Techniques) and US 7 (4.5mm) straight needles, CO 39 sts in colour A.

Row 2 K all sts.

Row 3 K all sts.

Row 4 K all sts.

Row 5 *K2, p1* repeat from * to end.

Row 6 *K1, p2* repeat from * to end.

Row 7 *K2, p1* repeat from * to end.

Row 8 K all sts.

Repeat rows 5–8, nine more times to row 34. Transfer work onto one of the DPNs. Once both parts of the base are knitted, split the sts onto three DPNs and join to start working in the round. (78 sts)

Round 36 K all sts.

Round 37 P all sts.

Round 38 K all sts.

Round 39 P all sts.

Round 40 (dec) *K2tog, k4* repeat from * to end. (65 sts)

Round 41 K all sts.

Round 42 (dec) Change to colour B. *K2tog, k3* repeat from * to end. (52 sts)

Round 43 K all sts.

Round 44 K all sts.

Round 45 K all sts.

Round 46 (dec) *K2tog, k2* repeat from * to end. (39 sts)

Round 47 K all sts.

Round 48 K all sts.

Round 49 (dec) *K2tog, k1* repeat from * to end. (26 sts)

Round 50 K all sts.

Round 51 K all sts.

Round 52 (dec) K2tog to end. (13 sts)

Round 53 K all sts.

Round 54 K all sts.

BO

WHEN YOU ARE WORKING IN THE ROUND YOU DON'T NEED TO PURL EVERY OTHER ROW TO CREATE STOCKING STITCH. YOU CAN KNIT EVERY ROW.

OWLS

Make 3

Using the long-tail CO method (see Techniques) and US 7 (4.5mm) DPNs, CO 3 sts in colour C. Join to work in the round and split across 3 DPNs.

Round 2 (inc) Kfb to end. (6 sts)

Round 3 K all sts.

Round 4 (inc) Kfb to end. (12 sts)

Round 5 K all sts.

Round 6 (inc)*Kfb, k1* repeat from * to end. (18 sts)

Work 6 rounds in st st.

Round 13 (inc) *Kfb, k2* repeat from * to end. (24 sts)

Work 6 rounds in st st.

Round 20 (dec) *K2tog, k2* repeat from * to end. (18 sts)

Round 21 (dec) *K2tog, k1* repeat from * to end. (12 sts)

Add the stuffing. Break yarn, leaving a long tail, thread through remaining live stitches and pull through. Weave in ends.

THE LEAVES

CO 2 sts in colour D and US 6 (4mm) straight needles.

Row 1 K all sts.

Row 2 P all sts.

Row 3 K all sts.

Row 4 P all sts.

Row 5 K all sts.

Row 6 P all sts.

Row 7 (inc) Kfb, k1. (3 sts)

Row 8 P all sts.

Row 9 (inc) Kfb, place the last 2 sts on a stitch holder.

Row 10 P all sts.

Row 11 K all sts.

Row 12 P all sts.

Row 13 (inc) [Kfbf] x 2. (6 sts)

Row 14 P all sts.

Row 15 (inc) Kfb, k4, kfb. (8 sts)

Row 16 P all sts.

Row 17 K all sts.

Row 18 P all sts.

Row 19 BO 2 sts, k6. (6 sts)

Row 20 BO 2 sts purlwise, p4. (4 sts)

Row 21 K all sts.

Row 23 (dec)[K2tog] x 2. (2 sts)

Row 24 BO purlwise.

Pick up the 2 sts placed on the stitch holder at row 9. K across.

Work 5 rows in st st.

Row 15 (inc) K1, kfb. (3 sts)

Row 16 P all sts.

Row 17 (inc) K2, kfb. (4 sts)

Row 18 P2. Place the remaining 2 sts on a stitch holder.

Row 19 K all sts.

Row 20 P all sts.

Row 21 K all sts.

Row 22 P all sts.

Row 23 K all sts.

Row 24 P all sts.

Row 25 (inc) [Kfbf] x 2. (6sts)

Row 26 P all sts.

Row 27 K all sts.

Row 28 P all sts.

Row 29 (inc) Kfb, k4, kfb. (8 sts)

Row 30 P all sts.

Row 31 BO 2 sts, k6. (6 sts)

Row 32 BO 2 purlwise, p4. (4 sts)

Row 33 K all sts.

Row 34 P all sts.

Row 35 (dec) [K2tog] x 2. (2 sts)

Row 36 P all sts.

Row 37 (dec) K2tog.

Break yarn, leaving a long tail, thread through remaining live sts and pull through. Weave in ends.

Pick up the 2 sts placed on stitch holder at row 18. P across.

Repeat rows 1–37.

Make 10 leaves and then reattach at row 18 on the ninth leaf and knit. Then work another 5 rows in st st.

Work rows 13–24 for the final leaf.

THE TOP OF THE NEST

CO 6 sts in colour A and work in garter st until the piece measures 46in (116cm). Bind of. Fold in half horizontally and sew up.

MAKING UP

Block your tea cosy. Weave in ends.

All teapots vary, so measure where the spout and handles start on your teapot. Sew up seams to these points.

Take the top of the nest and lay it so that the CO and BO edges are together. Sew up the CO and BO edges. Twist the piece around itself to create a new line piece. Place the new ends together and sew up. Then place the newly formed circle onto the top of the teapot, sitting before the start of colour B. Sew neatly into place.

EXTRA SEWING MAY BE NEEDED BETWEEN THE GAPS AT THE TOP OF THE SPOUT AND THE HANDLE.

THE OWLS

Stitch a few 'V's in the front of the owls using colour A to make them cuter.

Cut two beaks out of mustard felt using the owl beak template as a guide (see Templates). Cut six eyes out of the grey felt using the outer eye template. Cut six eyes in black felt from the inner eye template.

Using scrap cream DK yarn cut six ⅝in (1.5cm) pieces for the eyebrows.

Assemble the owls' faces as directed. Place the beak in the centre of the owl's face with the point of it 1¼ in (3cm) from the base, then the eyes either side with a ¼in (5mm) gap between. Sew the blacks of the eyes in the centre of the outer pieces using black thread or strong fabric glue. If sewing use the black thread and sew directly into the owls. Using mustard cotton carefully sew on the beak. Or alternatively glue all pieces on. Place the eyebrows ½in (1cm) from the top, its up to you how you'd like them to sit as they'll add all the character to your owls. Use a small amount of white cotton to securely sew the brows on.

Put the tea cosy onto the teapot, with the top of the lid through the hole. Then place your owls onto one side of it. Sew them on.

TRY PLACING THE EYEBROWS IN DIFFERENT WAYS TO ADD CHARACTER TO YOUR OWLS. DON'T FORGET TO SEW LITTLE 'V'S INTO THEM FOR ADDED DETAIL.

Additional sewing up may be needed between the top of the spout and where the two pieces were joined together

Sew up to the start of the spout

Sew up to the start of the handle

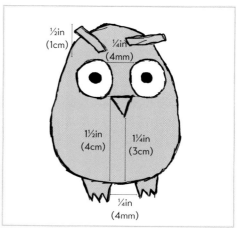

½in (1cm)

¼in (4mm)

1½in (4cm)

1¼in (3cm)

¼in (4mm)

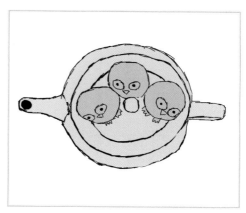

PHEASANT

SKILL LEVEL
BEGINNER

This Pheasant is easy to make and knits up really quickly with the super bulky yarn, so you'll have a kitchen full of them before you know it!

MATERIALS

A Erika Knight, Maxi Wool, Canvas x 1 ball (87 yards/80 metres per 100g)

B Erika Knight, Maxi Wool, Artisan x 1 ball (87 yards/80 metres per 100g)

C Erika Knight, Maxi Wool, Marni x 1 ball (87 yards/80 metres per 100g)

D Rowan, Thick 'n' Thin, Marble x 2 balls (54 yards/49 metres per 50g)

E Rowan, Thick 'n' Thin, Dolomite x 1 ball (54 yards/49 metres per 50g)

F Rowan, Thick 'n' Thin, Granite x 2 balls (54 yards/49 metres per 50g)

US 13 (9mm) straight needles

1¼in (37g) toy stuffing

Pheasant leg template (see Templates)

4¼ x 1½in (11 x 3.5cm) grey felt

Grey cotton

2 ½ in (10mm) black safety toy eyes

DIMENSIONS

26 x 4½in (67 x 12 cm)

GAUGE (TENSION)

10 sts and 13 rows to 4in (10cm) over st st

KNITTING TECHNIQUES

Long-tail cast on

Mattress stitch

Backstitch

PHEASANT BODY

Using the long-tail CO method (see Techniques) and US 13 (9mm) needles, CO 3 sts in colour A. This will make up the 1st row.

Row 2 P all sts.

Row 3 (inc) Kfb across all sts. (6 sts)

Row 4 P all sts.

Row 5 (inc) Change to colour E and *kfb, k1* repeat from * to end. (9 sts)

Row 6 P all sts.

Row 7 (inc) *Kfb, k2* to end. (12 sts)

Row 8 P all sts.

Row 9 (inc) *Kfb, k3* repeat from * to end. (15 sts)

Row 10 P all sts.

Row 11 K all sts.

Row 12 P all sts.

Row 13 (dec) Change to colour A and *k2tog, k3* repeat from * to end. (12 sts)

Row 14 K all sts.

Row 15 K all sts.

Row 16 K all sts.

Row 17 Change to colour D and k all sts.

Row 18 P all sts.

Row 19 (inc) *Kfb, k2* repeat from * to end. (16 sts)

Row 20 P all sts.

Row 21 (inc) *Kfb, k3* repeat from * to end. (20 sts)

Row 22 P all sts.

Row 23 (inc) *Kfb, k4* repeat from * to end. (24 sts)

Row 24 P all sts.

Row 25 (inc) *Kfb, k5* repeat from * to end. (28 sts)

Row 26 P all sts.

Row 27 (inc) *Kfb, k6* repeat from * to end. (32 sts)

Row 28 P all sts.

Row 29 (inc) *Kfb, k7* repeat from * to end. (36 sts)

Row 30 P all sts.

Row 31 (inc) *Kfb, k8* repeat from * to end. (40 sts)

Work 17 rows in st st.

Row 49 (dec) *K2tog, k2* repeat from * to end. (30 sts)

Row 50 P all sts.

Row 51 (dec) *K2tog, k1* repeat from * to end. (20 sts)

Row 52 P all sts.

Row 53 (dec) K2tog to end. (10 sts)

Row 54 P all sts.

Row 55 (dec) K2tog to end. (5 sts)

Row 56 P all sts.

Break yarn, leaving a long tail, thread through remaining live sts and pull through. Weave in ends.

WINGS

Make 4

Using the long-tail CO method (see Techniques) and US 13 (9mm) needles, CO 3 sts in colour F. This will make up the 1st row.

Row 2 P all sts.

Row 3 (inc) K1, kfb, k1. (4 sts)

Row 4 P all sts.

Row 5 (inc) K1, [kfb] x 2, k1. (6 sts)

Row 6 P all sts.

Row 7 (inc) K1, kfb, k2, kfb, k1. (8 sts)

Row 8 P all sts.

Row 9 (inc) K1, kfb, k4, kfb, k1. (10 sts)

Row 10 P all sts.

Row 11 (inc) K1, kfb, k6, kfb, k1. (12 sts)

Row 12 P all sts.

Row 13 (inc) K1, kfb, k8, kfb, k1. (14 sts)

Work 9 rows in st st.

Row 23 (dec) K1, k2tog, k8, k2tog, k1. (12 sts)

Row 24 P all sts.

Row 25 (dec) K1, k2tog, k6, k2tog, k1. (10 sts)

Row 26 P all sts.

Row 27 (dec) K1, k2tog, k4, k2tog, k1. (8 sts)

Row 28 P all sts.

Row 29 (dec) K1, k2tog, k2, k2tog, k1. (6 sts)

Row 30 P all sts.

BO

STRIPED LONG TAIL

Using the long-tail CO method (see Techniques) and US 13 (9mm) needles, CO 6 sts in colour B. This will make up the 1st row.

Row 2 P all sts.

Work 2 rows in st st.

Row 5 (inc) *Kfb, k1* to end. (9 sts)

Work 3 rows in st st.

Row 9 K to end in colour D.

Row 10 P all sts.

Row 11 Change to colour B and k to end.

Repeat rows 9–11, three more times.

Row 20 (dec) Change to colour D. *K2tog, k1* repeat from * to end. (6 sts)

Row 21 P all sts.

Row 23 Change to colour B and k to end.

Row 24 P all sts.

Row 25 Change to colour D and k to end.

Row 26 P all sts.

Row 27 Change to colour B and k to end.

Row 28 P all sts.

Row 29 (dec) Change to colour D and k2tog to end. (3 sts)

Row 30 P all sts.

Row 31 Change to colour B and k to end.

Row 32 P all sts.

Break yarn, leaving a long tail, thread through remaining live sts and pull through. Weave in ends.

SHORT PLAIN TAIL

Make 1 in colour D and 1 in colour B.

Using the long-tail CO method (see Techniques) and US 13 (9mm) needles, CO 6 sts.

Work 28 rows in st st.

Row 29 (dec) K2tog across all sts. (3 sts)

Work 5 rows in st st.

Break yarn, leaving a long tail, thread through remaining live sts and pull through. Weave in ends.

FOR THE SECOND COLOUR WAY MAKE SURE THE DARKER BLUE IS ON THE INSIDE OF THE WING.

THE RED EYE PANELS

Make 2

Using the long-tail CO method (see Techniques) and US 13 (9mm) needles, CO 3 sts in colour C. This will make up the 1st row.

Row 2 P all sts.

Row 3 (inc) K1, kfb, k1. (4 sts)

Row 4 P all sts.

Row 5 K all sts.

Row 6 BO purlwise.

FOR THE SECOND COLOUR WAY USE ONE WING PIECE IN COLOUR F AND ONE IN COLOUR E.

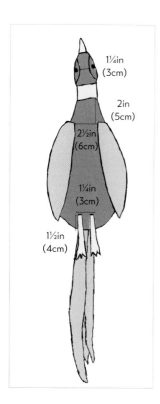

1¼in (3cm)

2in (5cm)

2½in (6cm)

1¼in (3cm)

1½in (4cm)

KNIT THEM UP QUICK AND USE AS MANY DIFFERENT COLOURS AS POSSIBLE! BUT BE CAREFUL NOT TO OVER STUFF.

MAKING UP

Use mattress stitch (see Techniques) to sew up the pheasant body, using the correct colours. Take two wings and place them with the RS facing in. Sew up using backstitch (see Techniques) and leaving the BO edges open. Turn inside out and sew up the opening.

Cut two feet in grey felt from the template. Place the two eyes in the centre of the red eye panels. Place the pheasant flat and pin the eye panels onto the blue part of the head, with a 1¼in (3cm) gap between them, and sew up. Using this as the centre, pin the wings 2in (5cm) from the white garter section with 2¼in (5.5cm) between them and, sew up using the grey cotton.

Following the centre line, place the feet 1½in (4cm) from the bottom of the pheasant with a 1¼in (3cm) gap between them. The tails should be pinned and sewn in the centre of the underneath of the pheasant (where the stitches were threaded through).

TRY CHANGING THE BEAK
COLOUR (A) TO B FOR ROWS
1–4 OF THE PHEASANT BODY.
MAKE TWO WINGS IN F
AND TWO IN E.

MOLE DOOR STOP

SKILL LEVEL
BEGINNER

Functional and fun, the Mole Door Stop is a great way
to add a bit of country heritage to your home. He'll be at
home amongst your Barbour-style jackets and wellington
boots, but could be used anywhere around the house!

MATERIALS

A Garthenor Organic Pure Wool,
Hebridean/Manx Loghtan blend
chunky, Chocoate/Black x 1 ball
(121 yards/111 metres per 100g)

B Garthenor Organic Pure Wool,
Hebridean/Manx Loghtan blend
chunky, Chocolate Brown x 1 ball
(121 yards/111 metres per 100g)

C Two strands of Jamieson & Smith,
Shetland Supreme, Yuglet x 1 ball
(188 yards/172 metres per 50g)

D Two strands of Jamieson & Smith,
Shetland Heritage, Flugga White x 1
ball (120 yards/110 metres per 25g)

E Jamieson & Smith, Shetland
Heritage, Berry Wine x 1 ball
(120 yards/110 metres per 25g)

US 10 (6mm) DPNs

US 6 (4mm) DPNs

A pair of tights

1lb 12oz (800g) of rice

¼oz (10g) stuffing

Mole feet template (see Templates)

Mole eye template (see Templates)

1½ x 1½in (4 x 4cm) baby pink felt
per foot

½ x ¼in (1 x 0.5cm) black felt per eye

A small amount of 35 lbs fishing wire
(Fladen Vantage .55)

DIMENSIONS

10 x 6½in (25 x 17cm)

GAUGE (TENSION)

12 sts and 16 rows to 4in (10cm) over
st st on larger needles

18 sts and 28 rows to 4in (10cm) over
st st on smaller needles

KNITTING TECHNIQUES

Long-tail cast on

THE MOUND AND MOLE

Using the long-tail CO method
(see Techniques) and US 10 (6mm)
needles, CO 48 sts in colour A. This
will make up the 1st round.

Work in st st for 17 rounds.

Round 19 (dec) *K2tog, k2* repeat
from * to end. (36 sts)

Round 20 K all sts.

Round 21 Change to colour B and
p all sts.

Round 22 K all sts.

Round 23 P all sts.

Round 24 K all sts.

Round 25 P all sts.

Round 26 K all sts.

Round 27 Change to US 8 (4mm)
DPNs and k all sts in colour C.

Work in st st for 8 rounds.

Round 36 (dec) K15, [k2tog] x 3,
k15. (33 sts)

Round 37 K all sts.

Round 38 K all sts.

Round 39 K all sts.

Round 40 (dec) K13, [k2tog] x 3,
k14. (30 sts)

Round 41 K all sts.

Round 42 K all sts.

Round 43 K all sts.

Round 44 (dec) K14, k2tog, k14.
(29 sts)

Round 45 K all sts.

Round 46 K all sts.

Round 47 K all sts.

Round 48 (dec) *K2tog, k2* repeat
from * to end. (21 sts)

Round 49 K all sts.

Round 50 (dec) *K2tog, k1* repeat
from * to end. (14 sts)

Round 51 K all sts.

Round 52 K all sts.

Round 53 K all sts.

Round 54 K all sts.

Round 55 K all sts.

Round 56 K all sts.

Round 57 Change to colour D and
k all sts.

Round 58 K all sts.

Round 59 K all sts.

Round 60 (dec) K2tog to end. (7 sts)

Round 61 K all sts.

Round 62 K all sts.

Round 63 BO all sts and weave in
the ends.

THE BASE OF THE MOUND

Using the long-tail CO method (see Techniques) and US 10 (6mm) DPNs, CO 60 sts in colour B. This will make up the 1st round.

Round 2 (dec) *K2tog, k4* repeat from * to end. (50 sts)

Round 3 K all sts.

Round 4 (dec) *K2tog, k3* repeat from * to end. (40 sts)

Round 5 K all sts.

Round 6 (dec) *K2tog, k2* repeat from * to end. (30 sts)

Round 7 K all sts.

Round 8 (dec) *K2tog, k1* repeat from * to end. (20 sts)

Round 9 K all sts.

Round 10 (dec) *K2tog* to end. (10 sts)

Round 11 K all sts.

Round 12 (dec) *K2tog* to end. (5 sts)

Break yarn, leaving a long tail, and thread through remaining live sts. Weave in ends.

MAKING UP

Block your mole. Weave in the ends. Turn the mound and mole inside out and pin the base circle, RS facing in, onto the CO edge. Sew up ¾ of the way around the circle. Turn the piece inside out so the RS is now facing out.

Take the pair of tights and cut 12in (30cm) from the bottom of the foot. Fill with the rice and tie a knot to secure.

Place ¼oz (8g) of stuffing into the mole's head. Then place the tights into the mound and add the extra stuffing around it.

Sew up the last ¼.

The mole will naturally fall one way so add a small st ¾in (2cm) under the mole's chin and into the mound. This will secure the mole into place.

Using colour E, embroider a small nose onto the top of the mole. Ensure that you cover the CO and first increased stitches.

WHISKERS

Using the fishing wire, sew into the white of the mole. Where the wire exits the mole sew it back into the head and out again to secure it. Do this twice on either side of the mole.

Cut two mole hands using the template and pink felt, and cut two eyes using the template and the black felt (see Templates).

Place the hands between the garter top and the start of the mole, leaving a 2in (5cm) gap between them. The hands will sit nicely over the garter top.

Place the eyes 1½ (4cm) away from the edge of the embroidered nose, leaving a ½ (1cm) gap in the centre between them.

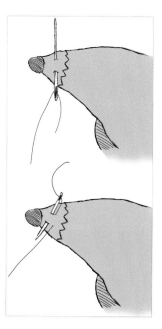

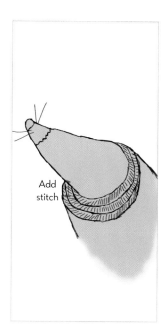

Add stitch

TIGER RUG

SKILL LEVEL
ADVANCED

Considering the size of this magnificent beast, he knits

up quite quickly by using two strands of super-bulky

yarn. Use a bright orange yarn for a vibrant pop of

colour or, if you're after a subtle colour scheme, you

could swap the orange for white.

MATERIALS

A 2 strands of Wool and the Gang, Crazy Sexy Wool, Fireball Orange x 10 balls (87 yards/80 metres per 200g)

B 2 strands of Wool and the Gang, Crazy Sexy Wool, Ivory White x 3 balls (87 yards/80 metres per 200g)

C 2 strands of Wool and the Gang, Crazy Sexy Wool, Space Black x 4 balls (80 yards/80 metres per 200g)

US 19 (15mm) straight or circular needles

Mustard felt 1½ x 1½in (4 x 4cm) x 2

Black felt 3¼ x 3¼in (8 x 8cm)

⅛in (24mm) black toy safety eyes

Black cotton or fabric glue

4½oz (125g) toy stuffing

Tiger eyes and nose template (see Templates)

A small amount of chunky black yarn

1½oz (40g) cream felting yarn

DIMENSIONS

50 x 61in (127 x 156cm)

GAUGE (TENSION)

6 sts and x 7 rows to 4in (10cm) over st st with 2 strands held together

KNITTING TECHNIQUES

Long-tail cast on

Intarsia

GETTING STARTED

The pattern has been displayed in chart form. CO 4 sts using the long-tail CO method (see Techniques), 2 strands of colour B and US 19 (15mm) needles.

These will make up the 1st row. The 2nd row, and all even rows will be purl rows. The top has a slightly different shaped face to the bottom, but both patterns start the same way.

In the pattern you will CO sts from edges sts, this will be done on the knit side and also on the purl side. The pattern is also BO on the knit and purl sides.

LEGS AND TAIL

It is recommended that you purl the 14 sts on row 92, BO the next 6 sts, work the tail, BO the next 6 sts and work

the other leg. Work the knit row as directed for row 93 and place the tail and other leg sts on a holder. Re-attach

these and work the tail once the leg has been finished, then work the other leg once the tail has been finished.

EARS

Make 2 in colour B and 2 in colour C

CO 5 sts using the long-tail CO method, 2 strands of yarn and US 19 (15mm) needles. This will make up the 1st row.

Row 2 P all sts.

Row 3 (inc) Kfb, k3, kfb. (7 sts)

Row 4 P all sts.

Row 5 K all sts.

Row 6 P all sts.

Row 7 (dec) K2tog, k3, k2tog. (5 sts)

Row 8 P all sts.

Row 9 Break yarn leaving a long tail. Thread through the sts, pull and weave in.

MAKING UP

Take the top piece of the Tiger and place it on to the bottom, with the WS facing in. Sew up using mattress stitch (see Techniques), making sure it is very neat. Sew the whole piece in the corresponding colours, but leave the head unsewn.

TRY KNITTING THE BOTTOM OF THE TIGER IN A DIFFERENT COLOUR, SUCH AS BLACK, IF YOU'RE WORRIED ABOUT THE ORANGE GETTING DIRTY.

THE FUR

For the fur use either unspun cream felting wool or you can use a little extra Wool and the Gang yarn as it easily pulls apart to create the same fluffy effect.

Take 1½oz (40g) of the felting wool and cut 3¼in (8cm) lengths of it, place it 1½in (4cm) from the CO edges, having enough to cover 8in (20cm) of the side of the tiger's head. Then place it between the 2 head pieces, leaving 2in (5cm) of it out and 1¼in (3cm) in the head. Sew up carefully using mattress stitch, leaving the front of the snout open. Repeat for the other side of the face.

THE FACE

Cut two eyes from the mustard felt, cutting a slit in the middle. Place the toy eye into the felt. Then place them 3½ in (9cm) from the start of colour A on the face, with a US 2¼ in (5.5cm) gap in the centre between them. They will sit nicely on the black stripes knitted on the face. You can use several strands of fluff for this and add more if you like, get creative!

The eyebrows are created using a similar method to the fur on the sides. Use 2in (5cm) strands of fur and place them 1¼ in (3cm) into the tiger's head, leaving ¾ in (2cm) of it out. These will be placed directly above the eyes running 2in (5cm) wide. It will be easy to push through the head, as the stitches are large. Tie the 1¼ in (3cm) of fur into knots to secure them. Pull the strands a little on the RS of the head if needed to bring them back to ¾ in (2cm).

Take one ear piece in colour B and 1 in colour C. Pin and sew together with mattress stitch. Then place a small handful of stuffing inside. Repeat for the second ear. Then place the ears 8¼ in (21cm) from the base of the nose, leaving an 4¼ in (11cm) gap in the centre between them. Have the colour B side facing forward. Sew neatly into the head using the corresponding colours.

Repeat the technique for the eyebrows, cutting them 3¼ in (8cm) long and placing them so 1½ in (4cm) are showing along a 2in (5cm) width next to the ear. Here strands of fur were used, alongside a strand or 2 of colour A.

Cut a nose from the black felt and place it in position, ¾in (2cm) from the base. Using the chunky black yarn add a few spots either side of the nose and a ¾in (2cm) stripe under the nose. Sew up using black cotton or secure in place with fabric glue.

Add the 4½oz (125g) stuffing to the tiger head and sew up the remaining areas needed. Place the stuffing evenly, shaping the face.

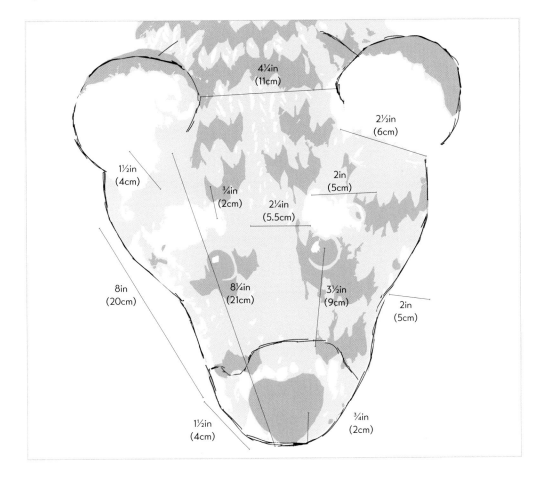

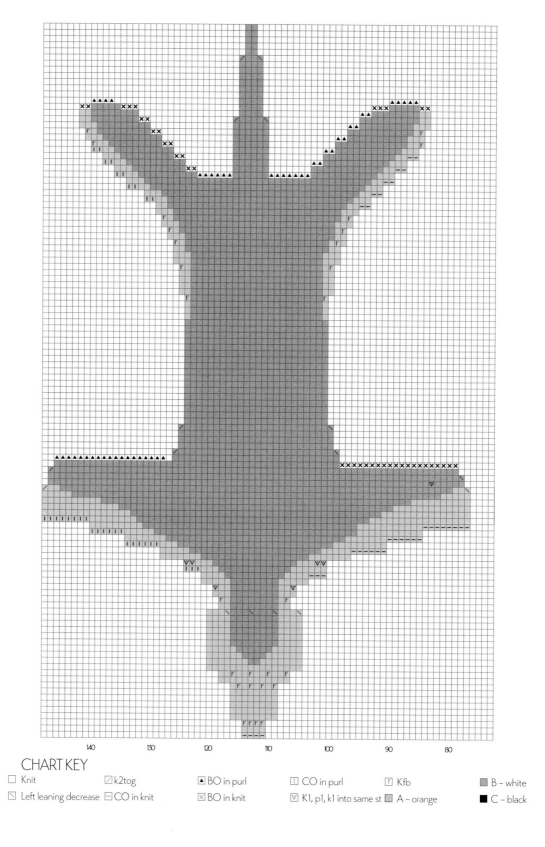

CHART KEY

☐ Knit	☑ k2tog	▲ BO in purl
◺ Left leaning decrease	⊟ CO in knit	☒ BO in knit

☐ CO in purl	ⵛ Kfb	⬛ B – white
ⱴ K1, p1, k1 into same st	☐ A – orange	■ C – black

140 130 120 110 100 90 80

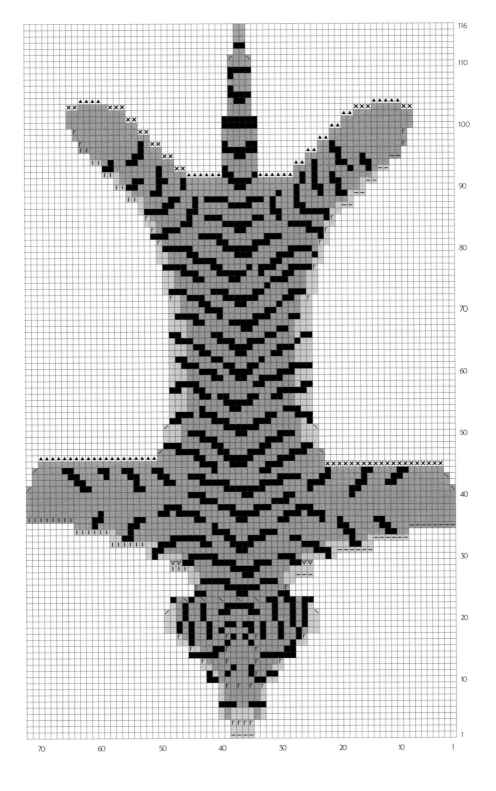

BADGER
HEAD

SKILL LEVEL
INTERMEDIATE

Bring badgers out of their setts and into the spotlight

with this rather dignified mounted badger head.

Monochrome is always on trend so you'll be sure to turn

heads with this trophy.

MATERIALS

A Rowan Creative Focus Worsted, Natural (220 yards/201 metres per 100g)

B Rowan Creative Focus Worsted, Ebony (220 yards/201 metres per 100g)

US 7 (4.5mm) straight needles

Toy stuffing

2 x 3.9in (10cm) black safety eyes

1¼in (3cm) black toy bobble

Black sewing thread

Badger template (see Templates)

7 x 7in (18 x 18cm) of ¹⁄₁₆in (2mm) cardboard

DIMENSIONS

HEAD: 8¼ x 4¼in (21 x 11cm)

EARS: 1¼ x 1¼in (3 x 3cm)

GAUGE (TENSION)

20 sts x 24 rows to 4in (10cm) over st st

KNITTING TECHNIQUES

Long-tail cast on

Intarsia

TOP OF BADGER HEAD

Using the long-tail CO method (see Techniques) and US 7 (4.5mm) needles, CO 6 sts in colour A.

Row 2 P all sts.

Row 3 (inc) Kfb all sts. (12 sts)

Row 4 P all sts.

Row 5 (inc) *Kfb, k1* repeat from * to end. (18 sts)

Row 6 P all sts.

Row 7 (inc) *Kfb, k2* repeat from * to end. (24 sts)

Work 7 rows in st st.

Row 15 K7a, k2b, k6a, k2b, k7a.

Row 16 P7a, p2b, p6a, p2b, p7a.

Row 17 (inc) K7a, [kfb] x 2 in B, k6a, [kfb] x 2 in B, k7a. (28 st)

Row 18 P7a, p4b, p6a, p4b, p7a.

Row 19 K7a, k4b, k6a, p4b, p7a.

Row 20 Repeat row 18.

Row 21 Repeat row 19.

Row 22 Repeat row 18.

Row 23 (inc) K7a, k1b, [kfb] x 2 in colour B, k1b, k6a, k1b, [kfb] x 2 in colour B, k1b, k7a. (32 sts)

Row 24 P7a, p6b, p6a, p6b, p7a.

Row 25 K7a, k6b, k6a, k6b, k7a.

Row 26 P7a, p6b, p6a, p6b, p7a.

Rep last 2 rows, 2 times.

Row 31 (inc) K7a, k1b, kfb in colour B, k2b, kfb in colour B, k1b, k6a, k1b, kfb in colour B, k2b, kfb in colour B, k1b, k7a. (36 sts)

Row 32 P7a, p8b, p6a, p8b, p7a.

Row 33 K7a, k8b, k6a, k8b, k7a.

Row 34 P7a, p8b, p6a, p8b, p7a.

Rep the last 2 rows 7 times.

Row 49 K7a, k9b, k4a, k9b, k7a.

Row 50 P7a, p9b, p4a, p9b, p7a.

Row 51 Repeat row 49.

Row 52 Repeat row 50.

Row 53 K7a, k10b, k2a, k10b, k7a.

Row 54 P7a, p10b, p2a, p10b, p7a.

Row 55 K6a, k11b, k2, k11b, k6a.

Row 56 P5a, p12b, p2a, p12b, p5a.

Row 57 K4a, k28b, k4a.

Row 58 P3a, p30b, p3a.

Row 59 K2a, k32b, k2a.

Row 60 P all sts in colour B.

Row 61 (dec) *K2tog, k4* repeat from * to end. (30 sts)

Row 62 P all sts.

Row 63 (dec) *K2tog, k3* repeat from * to end. (24 sts)

Row 64 P all sts.

Row 65 (dec) *K2tog, k2* repeat from * to end. (18 sts)

Row 66 P all sts.

Row 67 (dec) *K2tog, k1* repeat from * to end. (12 sts)

Row 68 P all sts.

BO

BOTTOM OF BADGER HEAD

Work rows 1–14 from the Top of the Badger Head.

Row 15 K all sts.

Row 16 P all sts.

Row 17 (inc) *Kfb, k5* repeat from * to end. (28 sts)

Work 4 rows in st st.

Row 23 (inc) *Kfb, k6* repeat from * to end. (32 sts)

Row 24 P all sts.

Row 25 K14a, k4b, k14a.

Row 26 P12a, p8b, p12a.

Row 27 K10a, k12b, k10a.

Row 28 P8a, p16b, p8a.

Row 29 K8a, p16b, p8a.

Row 30 Repeat row 28.

Row 31 (inc) Kfb in colour A, k7a, [kbf in colour B, k7b] x2, kfb in colour A, k7a. (36 sts)

Row 32 P9a, p18b, p9a.

Row 33 K7a, k22b k7a.

Row 34 P5a, p26b, p5a.

Row 35 K3a, k30b, k3a.

Row 36 P all sts in colour B, and work in colour B from here on.

Row 37 K all sts.

Row 38 P all sts.

Row 39 (inc) *Kfb, k5* repeat from * to end. (42 sts)

Row 40 P all sts.

Row 41 K all sts.

Row 42 P all sts.

Row 43 (inc) *Kfb, k6* repeat from * to end. (48 sts)

Row 44 P all sts.

Row 45 K all sts.

Row 46 P all sts.

Row 47 (inc) *Kfb, k7* repeat from * to end. (54 sts)

Row 48 P all sts.

Row 49 K all sts.

Row 50 P all sts.

Row 51 (inc) *Kfb, k8* repeat from * to end. (60 sts)

Row 52 P all sts.

Row 53 K all sts.

Row 54 P all sts.

Row 55 (inc) *Kfb, k9* repeat from * to end. (66 sts)

Work 13 rows in st st.

BO

EARS

Make 2 in colour A and 2 in colour B.

Using the long-tail CO method (see Techniques) and (US 7) 4.5mm needles, CO on 8 sts.

Row 2 P all sts.

Row 3 K all sts.

Row 4 P all sts.

Row 5 K all sts.

Row 6 P all sts.

Row 7 K all sts.

Row 8 (dec) P3tog, p2, p3tog. (4 sts)

BO

MAKING UP

Weave in all the ends. Take the top and bottom piece of the Badger Head, with the RS facing in, and place the CO edges together. Pin all the way up each side to the BO edge. Sew up leaving the BO edge open. Turn inside out. Stuff lightly.

Place the black toy bobble 1¼in (3cm) from the bottom seam (the CO edges) and in the centre of the face. Sew on using black thread. Then measure 3¾in (9.5cm) from the bottom seam and 2 sts into the black (from the centre) on either side of the face, place the eyes here and secure.

Take an A ear and a B ear, with RS facing in, pin and sew together leaving the CO edge open. Place the ears 2¾in (7cm) from the bottom seam, on the edge of the black, 2in (5cm) from the side seam. Add a st ¼in (5mm) up on the back of the ear to ¼in (5mm) into the badger head to keep them in place.

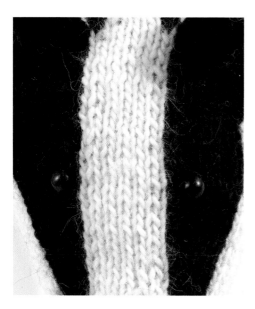

DON'T FORGET TO ADD THE EXTRA STUFFING NEEDED TO PAD OUT THE NECK, BUT BE CAREFUL NOT TO OVER STUFF

TEMPLATE INSTRUCTIONS

Cut out the template (see Templates) and place over 1/16in (2mm) thick cardboard. Draw around and cut out. With the template still over the cardboard, place pins into the marked holes.

Remove the pins and, using a big sewing needle, push into and through the holes. Place the back of the Badger Head against the cardboard, so the BO edge sits on the edge. Make sure it is sitting straight. Take a corresponding colour thread to the piece and sew into the first top hole.

Push through into the back of the head, pull the yarn but leave a tail. Sew the yarn back into the head, where the BO edge is sitting on the cardboard. Pull through and sew into the next hole.

Repeat this process anticlockwise around the head, but leave a gap on the last ¼.

Add extra stuffing for the neck of the badger and continue sewing up. Then repeat the same process anticlockwise. At the top hole of the board, make a small loop, tie securely and sew both ends in. Hang on a picture hook or nail.

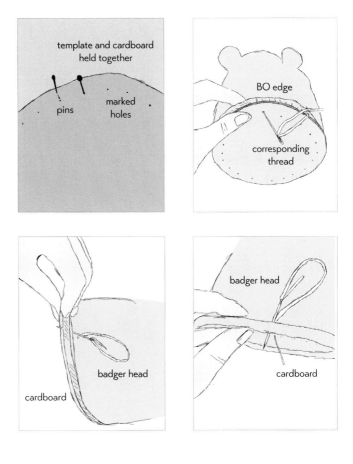

BEAR
COASTERS

SKILL LEVEL
BEGINNER

If you love the idea of a faux-skin rug but want to start

small, then these cute Bear Coasters are exactly what

you need. Plus, these tiny faux bear-skin rugs will protect

your furniture from unsightly coffee-stain rings!

MATERIALS

Drops Lima (98 yards/90 metres per 50g)
(in either Off White, Brown or Black)

US 6 (4mm) straight needles

Stitch holder

Fabric glue

¼in (5mm) diametre circles of black felt x 2

⅜in (4mm) diametre circle of black felt x 1

DIMENSIONS

7 x 6in (18 x 15cm)

GAUGE (TENSION)

21 sts x 28 rows to 4in (10cm) over st st

KNITTING TECHNIQUES

Long-tail cast on

Intarsia

BODY

Make 2

Using the long-tail CO method (see Techniques) and US 6 (4mm) straight needles, CO 4 sts. This will make up the 1st row.

Row 2 P all sts.

Row 3 (inc) Kfb, k2, kfb. (6 sts)

Row 4 P all sts.

Row 5 K all sts.

Row 7 (inc) *Kfb* repeat from * to end. (12 sts)

Row 6 P all sts.

Row 8 P all sts.

Row 9 (inc) *Kfb, k1* repeat from * to end. (18 sts)

Work 7 rows in st st.

Row 17 (dec) *K2tog, k1* repeat from * to end. (12 sts)

Row 18 P all sts.

Row 19 (dec) *K2tog* repeat from * to end. (6 sts)

Row 20 P all sts.

Row 21 (inc) [Kfbf] x 2, k to the last 2 sts, [kfbf] x 2. (14 sts)

Row 22 P all sts.

Repeat the last 2 rows 4 times. (46 sts)

Row 31 K all sts.

Row 32 P all sts.

Row 33 BO 13, k to end. (33 sts)

Row 34 BO 15 purlwise, p to end. (18 sts)

Work 6 rows in st st.

Row 41 (inc) Kfb, k to the last 2 sts, kfb. (20 sts)

Work in 5 rows in st st.

Row 47 (inc) Kfb, k to the last 2 sts, kfb. (22 sts)

Row 48 P all sts.

Row 49 K9, BO 6 sts, place 9 sts onto a stitch holder (this will become the right leg), continue working on the remaining 9 sts for the left leg.

LEFT LEG

Row 50 P all sts.

Row 51 BO 1 st, k to the end of the row. (8 sts)

Row 52 P all sts.

Row 53 BO 1 st, k to the last st, kfb. (8 sts)

Row 54 P all sts.

Repeat the last 2 rows.

Row 57 BO 1 st, k to the last 2 sts, k2tog. (6 sts)

Row 58 P all sts.

BO

RIGHT LEG

Row 50 Remove sts from stitch holder and reattach the yarn to the right leg. P all sts. (9 sts)

Row 51 K all sts.

Row 52 BO 1 st purlwise, p to the end of the row. (8 sts)

Row 53 (inc) Kfb, k to the end of the row. (9 sts)

Repeat the last 2 rows. (10 sts)

Row 56 BO 1 st purlwise, p to the end of the row. (9 sts)

Row 57 (dec) K2tog, k to the last 2 sts, k2tog. (7 sts)

Row 58 BO 1 st purlwise, p to the end of the row. (6 sts)

BO

EARS

Make 2

Using the long-tail CO method (see Techniques) and US 6 (4mm) straight needles, CO 6 sts in your chosen colour. This will make up the 1st row.

Row 2 P all sts.

Row 3 K all sts.

Row 4 P all sts.

Row 5 (dec) K2tog, k2, k2tog. (4 sts)

BO purlwise

MAKING UP

Weave in the ends. Place two parts of the body against each other with the RS facing in and pin. Sew up from the edge of the BO edge, all the way around, leaving the edge open.

Turn inside out and stuff the head. Push the stuffing into the edge of each foot. Neatly sew up the BO edge.

Place the ears 1¾in (4.5cm) from the bottom of the nose and about ½in (1cm) from the edge seam. Sew on.

Place the eyes about ¾in (2cm) from the bottom, just after the increased sts. Stick them on using fabric glue, applying some pressure for a minute or so.

Place the nose in the centre of the face, above the seam. Using fabric glue stick it on, applying some pressure for a minute or so.

A KNITTING NEEDLE WILL HELP POKE THE STUFFING THROUGH THE NECK AND INTO THE HEAD

ADDING STUFFING TO EACH PAW SHOULD HELP THE LEGS RAISE SLIGHTLY WHEN A CUP IS PLACED ON THE COASTER

TECHNIQUES

KNITTING ABBREVIATIONS

Abbreviations are used in knitting patterns to shorten commonly used terms so that the instructions are easier to read and a manageable length. The following is a list of the abbreviations you need to make the projects in this book. All knitting patterns in this book use UK terminology.

BO	bind off		p	purl
CO	cast on		psso	pass slipped stitches over
cm	centimetre(s)		p2tog	purl 2 stitches together (1 stitch decreased)
dec(s)	decrease/decreasing			
DK	double knitting		p3tog	purl 3 stitches together (2 stitches decreased)
DPNs	double-pointed needles		rep(s)	repeat(s)
g	gram(s)		RH	right hand
inc	increase(s)/increasing		rnd	round
in(s)	inch(es)		RS	right side
k	knit		sl	slip
k2tog	knit 2 stitches together (1 stitch decreased)		sl st	slip stitch
k3tog	knit 3 stitches together (2 stitches decreased)		SSK	slip, slip, knit
kfb	knit into front and back of stitch (1 stitch increased)		st st	stocking stitch (1 row k, 1 row p)
			st(s)	stitch(es)
kfbf	knit into front, back and front of stitch (2 stitches increased)		tog	together
			WS	wrong side
LH	left hand		yo	yarn over
m	metre(s)			
mm	millimetres			
M1	make one			
oz	ounces			

CASTING ON

To begin knitting, you need to work a foundation row of stitches and this is called casting on.

1 Take two needles and make a slip knot about 15cm (6in) from the end of the yarn on one needle. Hold this needle in your left hand. Insert the right-hand needle knitwise into the loop on the left-hand needle and wrap the yarn around the tip.

2 Pull the yarn through the loop to make a stitch but do not drop the stitch off the left-hand needle.

3 Slip the new stitch on to the left-hand needle by inserting the left-hand needle into the front of the loop from right to left. You will now have two stitches on the left-hand needle.

4 Insert the right-hand needle between the two stitches on the left-hand needle and wrap the yarn around the tip. Pull the yarn back through between the two stitches and place it on the left-hand needle, as in step 3. Repeat until you have cast on the required number of stitches.

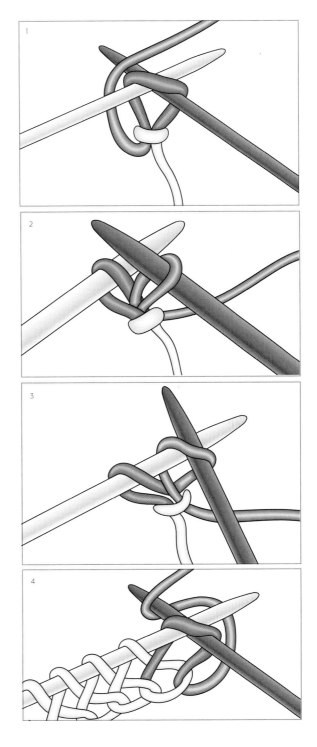

LONG-TAIL CAST ON

This is the simplest way of casting on and you will need only one needle.

1 Make a slip knot some distance from the end of the yarn and place it on the needle. Hold the needle in your right hand. Pass the ball end of the yarn over the index finger, under the middle and then over the third finger. Holding the free end of yarn in your left hand, wrap it around your left thumb from front to back.

2 Insert the needle through the thumb loop from front to back.

3 Wrap the ball end over the needle.

4 Pull a new loop through the thumb loop by passing the thumb loop over the end of the needle. Remove your thumb and tighten the new loop on the needle by pulling the free end. Continue in this way until you have cast on the required number of stitches.

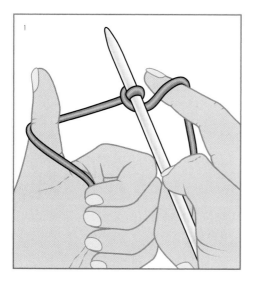

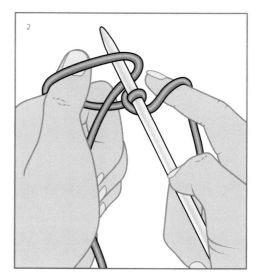

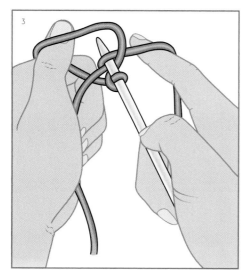

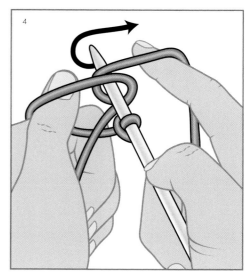

BINDING OFF

Binding off links stitches together to stop them from unravelling at the edge of a knitted fabric. There are a number of different ways to bind off.

BIND OFF KNITWISE

This is the easiest method to bind off on a knit row.

1 Knit two stitches, insert the tip of the left-hand needle into the front of the first stitch on the right-hand needle.

2 Lift this stitch over the second stitch and off the needle.

3 One stitch is left on the right-hand needle.

4 Knit the next stitch and lift the second stitch over this and off the needle. Continue in this way until one stitch remains on the right-hand needle.

TO FINISH

Cut the yarn (leaving a length long enough to sew in), thread the end through the last stitch and slip it off the needle. Pull the yarn end to tighten the stitch.

BIND OFF PURLWISE

To bind off on a purl row, simply purl the stitches instead of knitting them.

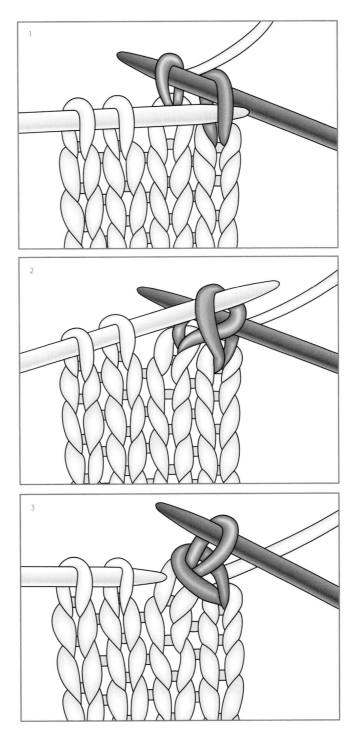

GAUGE (TENSION)

At the beginning of any knitting pattern the designer will state the gauge (tension) that you need to achieve and this is used to calculate the finished dimensions of the project. It is a very important part of knitting and is the number of stitches and rows to 4in (10cm). If you do not get the correct gauge (tension) the project will not be the correct size. More stitches to 4in (10cm) and the project will be smaller; fewer stitches to 4in (10cm) and the project will be bigger.

You must work a square of fabric measuring at least 6in (15cm), using the stated yarn, needle size and stitch. You can then measure the fabric in the middle of the square, avoiding the edge stitches as they will be distorted.

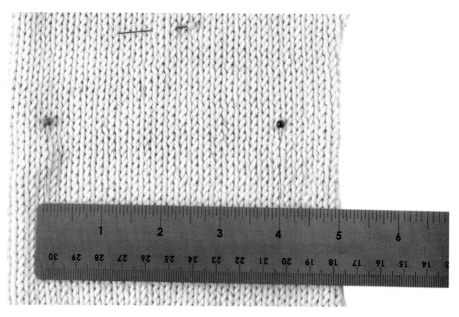

KNITTING A GAUGE (TENSION) SQUARE

To knit a gauge (tension) square for stocking stitch, cast on the number of stitches stated for 4in (10cm) plus 10 extra stitches.

1 Work in stocking stitch for at least 6in (15cm) and then bind off loosely.

2 Steam or block the square in the way that you will use for your finished project. The knitting pattern will tell you whether to block the pieces or not.

3 Lay the square on a flat surface without stretching it. Place a ruler horizontally on the square and place a pin four stitches in from the edge and place another at 4in (10cm) from the first pin.

4 Do the same for the rows by placing the ruler vertically, keeping away from the cast on and bind off edges, which may pull the fabric in.

5 Count the number of stitches and rows between the pins and this will be your gauge (tension).

Too many stitches means that your stitches are too small; you need to use a size larger needle to make the stitches bigger and so get fewer to 4in (10cm). Too few stitches means your stitches are too big; you need to

use a size smaller needle to make the stitches smaller and therefore get more to 4in (10cm).

6 Work more gauge (tension) squares with different-sized needle until you achieve the gauge (tension) stated in the pattern.

Checking your gauge (tension) will save you time spent unravelling your work and starting again. It also means the difference between a perfect project and a disaster!

KNIT STITCH (K)

This is the simplest stitch of all. Each stitch is created with a four-step process. Hold the yarn at the back of the work – this is the side facing away from you.

1 Place the needle with the cast-on stitches in your left hand, insert the right-hand needle into the front of the first stitch on the left-hand needle from left to right.

2 Take the yarn around and under the point of the right-hand needle.

3 Draw the new loop on the right-hand needle through the stitch on the left-hand needle.

4 Slide the stitch off the left-hand needle. This has formed one knit stitch on the right-hand needle.

Repeat until all stitches on the left-hand needle have been transferred to the right-hand needle. This is the end of the row. Swap the right-hand needle into your left hand and begin the next row in exactly the same way.

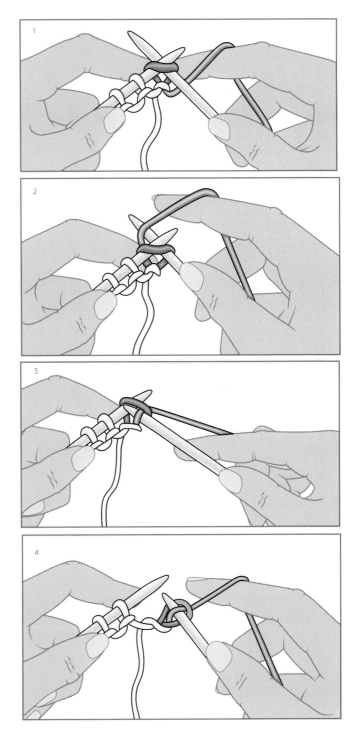

KNIT STITCH –
CONTINENTAL
METHOD

In this method the right-hand needle moves to catch the yarn; the yarn is held at the back of the work (the side facing away from you) and is released by the index finger of the left hand.

1 Hold the needle with the cast-on stitches in your left hand and the yarn over your left index finger. Insert the right-hand needle into the front of the stitch from left to right.

2 Move the right-hand needle down and across the back of the yarn.

3 Pull the new loop on the right-hand needle through the stitch on the left-hand needle, using the right index finger to hold the new loop if needed.

4 Slip the stitch off the left-hand needle. One knit stitch is completed.

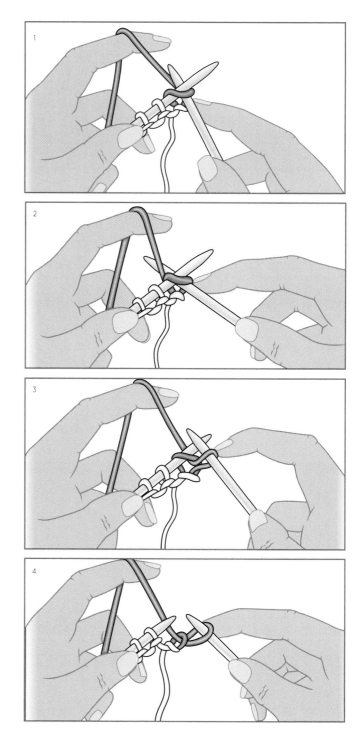

PURL STITCH (P)

This is the reverse of knit stitch. Hold the yarn at the front of the work – this is the side facing you.

1 Place the needle with the cast-on stitches in your left hand, insert the right-hand needle into the front of the first stitch on the left-hand needle from right to left.

2 Take the yarn over and around the point of the right-hand needle.

3 Draw the new loop on the right-hand needle through the stitch on the left-hand needle.

4 Slide the stitch off the left-hand needle. This has formed one purl stitch on the right-hand needle. Repeat these four steps to the end of the row.

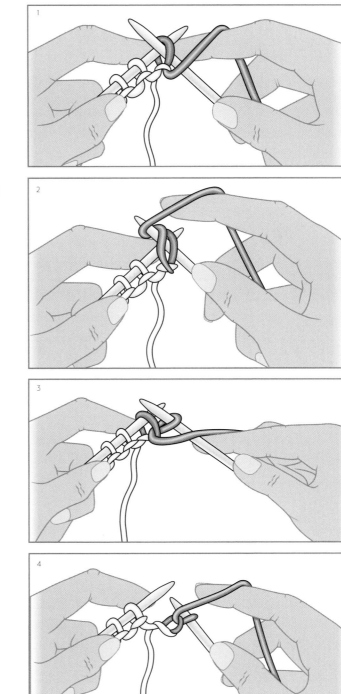

PURL STITCH – CONTINENTAL METHOD

Hold the yarn in your left hand, at the front of the work (the side facing you).

1 Hold the needle with the cast-on stitches in your left hand and insert the right-hand needle into the front of the stitch from right to left, keeping the yarn at the front of the work.

2 Move the right-hand needle from right to left behind the yarn, and then from left to right in front of the yarn. Pull your left index finger down in front of the work to keep the yarn taut.

3 Pull the new loop on the right-hand needle through the stitch on the left-hand needle, using the right index finger to hold the new loop if needed.

4 Slip the stitch off the left-hand needle. Return the left index finger to its position above the needle. One stitch is completed.

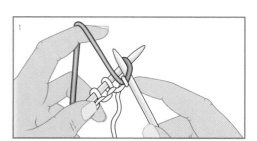

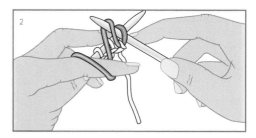

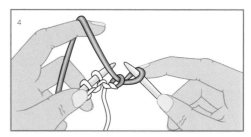

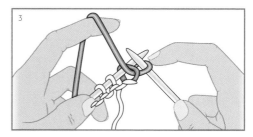

STOCKING STITCH (ST ST)

Stocking or stockinette stitch is formed by working alternate knit and purl rows. The knit rows are the right side of the fabric and the purl rows are the wrong side. Instructions for stocking stitch in knitting patterns can be written as follows:

Row 1 RS Knit

Row 2 Purl

Or alternatively: work in st st (1 row k, 1 row p), beg with a k row.

GARTER STITCH

When you knit each row the fabric you make is called garter stitch and has rows of raised ridges on the front and back of the fabric. It looks the same on both sides so it is reversible. Garter stitch lies flat, is quite a thick fabric and does not curl at the edges.

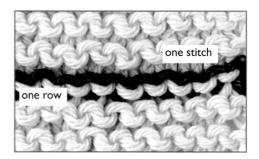

one stitch

one row

INCREASING STITCHES

Increasing stitches is a way of shaping the knitting and there are several methods.

MAKE 1 (M1) – TWIST M1 TO THE LEFT

A new stitch is made between two existing stitches using the horizontal thread that lies between the stitches.

1 Knit to the point where the increase is to be made. Insert the tip of the left-hand needle under the running thread from front to back.

2 Knit this loop through the back to twist it. By twisting it you prevent a hole appearing where the made stitch is.

MAKE 1 (M1) – TWIST M1 TO THE RIGHT

1 Knit to the point where the increase is to be made. Insert the tip of the left-hand needle under the running thread from back to front.

2 Knit this loop through the front to twist it.

KNIT INTO FRONT AND BACK (KFB)

An easy way to increase one stitch is by working into the front and back of the same stitch.

Knit into the front of the stitch as usual. Do not slip the stitch off the left-hand needle but knit into it again through the back of the loop, and then slip the original stitch off the left-hand needle. You can make a stitch on a purl row in the same way by purling into the front and back of the stitch (pfb).

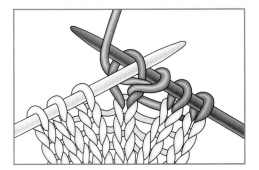

DECREASING STITCHES

As well as being able to increase stitches you will need to be able to decrease stitches for shaping. Stitches can be decreased singly or by several at once. Several methods are described here.

DECREASING ONE STITCH – KNIT 2 TOGETHER (K2TOG)

Knit to where the decrease is to be, insert the right-hand needle (as though to knit) through the next two stitches and knit them together as one stitch.

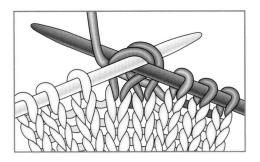

DECREASING ONE STITCH – PURL 2 TOGETHER (P2TOG)

Purl to where the decrease is to be, insert the right-hand needle (as though to purl) through the next two stitches and purl them together as one stitch.

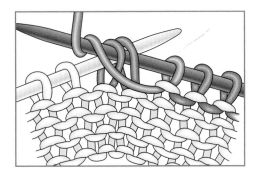

CIRCULAR KNITTING

DOUBLE-POINTED NEEDLES (DPN)

Flat knitting is knitted in rows, working back and forth, moving the stitches from one needle to the other. Circular knitting is knitted in rounds, working round and round without turning the work.

Use a set of four double-pointed needles, adding the stitches at one end and taking them off at the other. Cast the stitches on to one needle and then divide them evenly between three of the needles. For example, if you need to cast on 66 sts, there will be 22 sts on each needle; if you need to cast on 68 sts, there will be 23 sts on two of the needles and 22 on the third. The fourth needle is the working needle.

Arrange the needles into a triangle, making sure the cast on edge faces inwards and is not twisted. Place a marker between the last and first cast on stitches to identify the beginning of the round. Slip this marker on every round. Knit the first stitch, pulling up the yarn firmly so there is no gap between the third and first needle. Knit across the rest of the stitches on the first needle. As this needle is now empty, it becomes the working needle.

Knit the stitches from the second needle, then use the new working needle to knit the stitches from the third needle. One round has been completed.

Continue in this way, working in rounds and creating a tube of fabric. By knitting each round you will produce stocking stitch. To produce garter stitch, you will need to knit one round and then purl one round.

The first round is awkward; the needles not being used dangle and get in the way. When you have worked a few rounds the fabric helps hold the needles in shape and knitting will become easier.

To avoid a gap at the beginning of the first round, use the tail end of the yarn and the working yarn together to work the first few stitches. Or cast on one extra stitch at the end of the cast on, slip it on to the first needle and knit it together with the first stitch.

Avoid gaps at the change over between needles by pulling the yarn up tightly, or work a couple of extra stitches from the next needle on each round. This will vary the position of the change over and avoid a ladder of looser stitches forming.

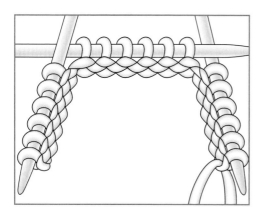

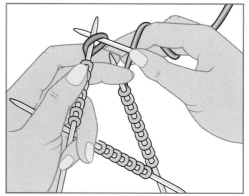

INTARSIA

Intarsia is a technique of colour knitting suitable for large areas of colour where several blocks of different colours are worked in the same row. Intarsia knitting is characterized by single motifs, geometric patterns or pictures.

Intarsia uses a separate ball of yarn for each block of colour. The yarns are twisted together to link the areas of colour and prevent a hole.

BOBBINS

Each area of colour needs its own bobbin of yarn. You should never knit straight from the ball because with all the twisting, the yarn will become horribly tangled and the knitting becomes a chore. Working with bobbins you can pull out sufficient yarn to knit the stitches and then leave it hanging at the back of the work out of the way of the other yarns.

You can buy plastic bobbins and wrap a small amount of yarn on to each one. But it is easy to make your own and cheaper if the intarsia design requires a lot of separate areas of colour. Leaving a long end, wind the yarn in a figure of eight around your thumb and little finger. Cut the yarn and use this cut end to tie a knot around the middle of the bobbin. Use the long end to pull the yarn from the middle of the bobbin. If the knotted end becomes loose around the bobbin as you pull yarn out, keep tightening it otherwise the bobbin will unravel.

Plan your knitting before you start. Work out how many bobbins of each colour you will need. If there are only a small number of stitches to be worked, cut a sufficient length of yarn, there is no need to wind it into a bobbin. Allow three times the width of stitches for the yarn needed to work those stitches.

BRINGING IN A NEW COLOUR

1 Insert the tip of the right-hand needle into the next stitch, place the cut end 4in (10cm) from the end of the new colour over the old colour and over the tip of the right-hand needle.

2 Take the working end of the new colour and knit the next stitch, pulling the cut end off the needle over the working end as the stitch is formed so it is not knitted in. Hold the cut end down against the back of the work.

The old and new colours will be twisted together, preventing a hole and you can carry on using the new colour. Leave the cut end dangling to be sewn in later or continue weaving it in.

On a purl row, join in a new colour in the same way, twisting the yarns together on the wrong side of the work.

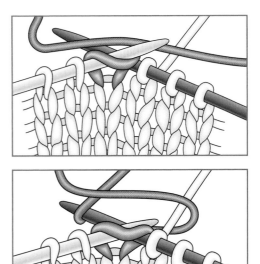

TWISTING YARNS TOGETHER

Once you've joined in all the colours that you need across the row, on the return row the yarns should be twisted to join the blocks of colour together. When you change colour, always pick up the new colour from under the old yarn. This is particularly important when the colours are changed at the same place in two or more rows. A line of loops will be formed on the wrong side of the work; these should not show through to the right side. Pull the yarns up firmly for the first stitch after twisting.

Twisting yarns on a knit row

Insert the tip of the right-hand needle into the next stitch, pull the old colour to the left, pick up the new colour and bring it up behind the old colour. Knit the next stitch. The two yarns are twisted together.

Twisting yarns on a purl row

Insert the tip of the right-hand needle into the next stitch, pull the old colour to the left, pick up the new colour and bring it up behind the old colour. Purl the next stitch. The two yarns are twisted together.

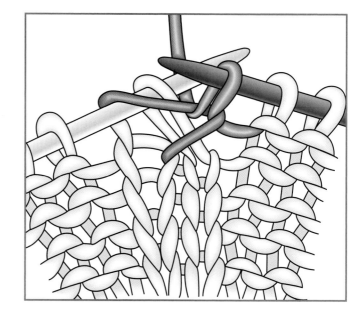

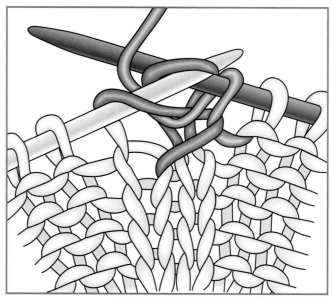

CARRYING YARN

Sometimes you will need to begin a new colour several stitches before where you used it on the previous row. Work the next stitch with the new colour, twisting it with the old colour as before; do not pull the yarn too tightly across the back of the work, spread the stitches out to get the correct tension. This will result in a loop of the new colour laying across the back of the work. If it is only a couple of stitches, this will not be a problem. If it is over several stitches, and there is a long loop, you need to catch it into the knitting or it will snag during wear. If it is more than seven stitches, it is best to cut the yarn and join it in at the new position.

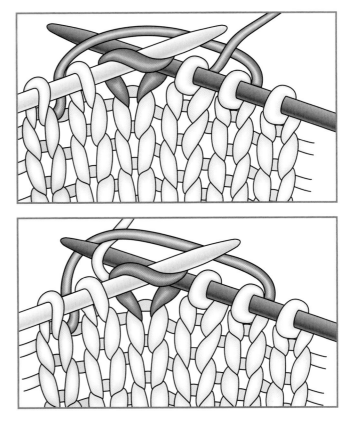

On a knit row

1 Knit two stitches in the new colour. Insert the tip of the right-hand needle into the next stitch, then pick up the long loop.

2 Wrap the yarn around as though you are going to knit, then pull the long loop off the needle. Knit the stitch. The loop will be caught without appearing on the front of the work.

On a purl row

1 Purl two stitches in the new colour. Insert the tip of the right-hand needle into the next stitch, then pick up the long loop.

2 Wrap the yarn around as though you are going to purl, then pull the long loop off the needle. Purl the stitch. The loop will be caught without appearing on the front of the work.

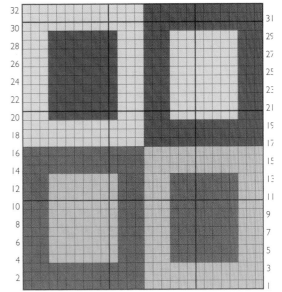

BINDING OFF

Binding off (casting off) links and secures stitches
together so that the knitting cannot unravel when
completed. Binding off is normally done following the
stitch sequence, so a knit stitch is bound off knitwise
and a purl stitch purlwise. Don't bind off too tightly as
this may pull the fabric in. To bind off on a purl row,
follow the Bind Off Knitwise steps but purl the
stitches instead of knitting them.

BIND OFF KNITWISE

1 Knit the first two stitches. Insert the point of the
left-hand needle into the front of the first stitch on the
right-hand needle.

2 Lift the first stitch on the right-hand needle over the
second stitch and off the needle. One stitch is left on
the right-hand needle.

3 Knit the next stitch on the left-hand needle, so
there are again two stitches on the right-hand needle.
Lift the first stitch on the right-hand needle over the
second stitch, as in step 2. Repeat this until one stitch
is left on the right-hand needle. Cut the yarn (leaving
a length long enough to sew in) and pass the end
through the last stitch. Slip the stitch off the needle
and pull the yarn end to tighten it.

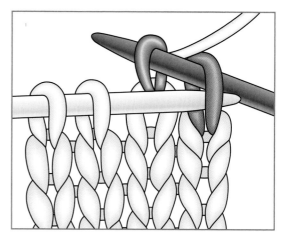

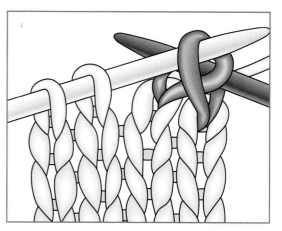

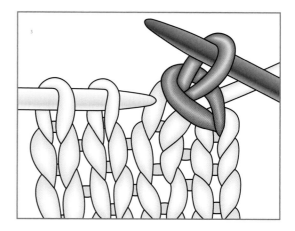

PICKING UP STITCHES

With the right side of the work facing, the needle is held in the right hand and inserted through the edge stitches, the left hand is holding the work. A new ball of yarn is joined and is wrapped around the needle and a loop is pulled through. One stitch has been knitted on to the needle. Use a size smaller needle than that used for the main piece of fabric.

ON A HORIZONTAL BOUND OFF EDGE

Hold the work in your left hand. With a needle and the yarn in your right hand, insert the needle into the centre of the first stitch in the row below the bound off edge. Wrap the yarn knitwise around the needle and draw through a loop. Continue in this way, inserting the needle through the centre of the stitch.

ON A VERTICAL EDGE

Hold the work in your left hand. With a needle and the yarn in your right hand, insert the needle between the first and second stitches at the beginning of the first row, wrap the yarn around knitwise and pull through a stitch. Continue up the edge, inserting the needle between the stitches on each row, taking in one stitch. If you are using a thick yarn, where one stitch may measure ½ in (1.5cm) or more, insert the needle through the centre of the edge stitch, taking in only half a stitch to reduce bulk.

DARNING IN ENDS

You will have some loose ends from casting on, binding off and changing colours and these can be woven into the knitting to secure them and create a neat look. Thread the loose end through a large-eyed tapestry or darning needle and pass the needle through the 'bumps' of the stitches on the back of the work for about 5cm (2in) and then snip off excess yarn.

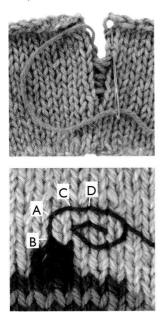

MATTRESS STITCH

To get an invisible seam use mattress stitch. This is worked from the right side, making it easier to match patterns. Place the two pieces to be joined side by side on a flat surface.

Secure the yarn by weaving it down the edge of one of the pieces, bringing it to the front on the first row between the corner stitch and the second stitch. On the opposite edge, insert the needle from back to front on the first row between the corner stitch and the second stitch. Take the needle back to the first edge and insert it from back to front through the same hole. Pull the yarn up tight to draw the pieces together.

BACKSTITCH

A continuous line used for outlining, for flower stems or for adding details. To begin bring the needle up at A. Take the needle down at B and then up at C, down at A and up at D.

TEMPLATES

Download printable templates at http://ideas.stitchcraftcreate.co.uk/patterns

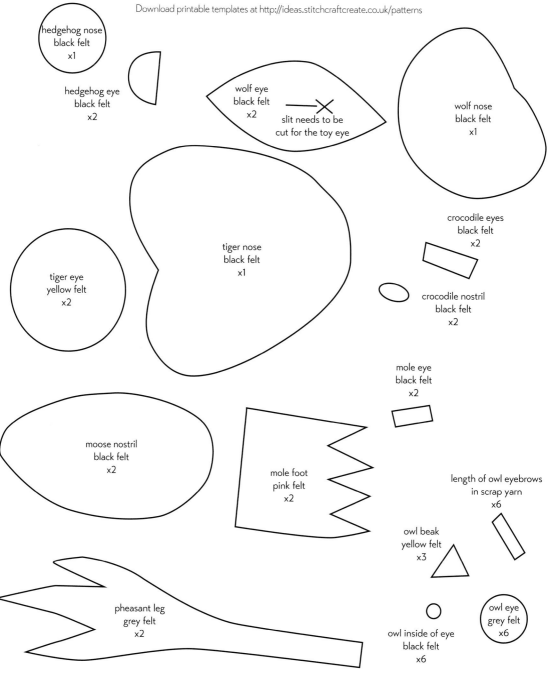

hedgehog nose
black felt
x1

hedgehog eye
black felt
x2

wolf eye
black felt
x2

slit needs to be
cut for the toy eye

wolf nose
black felt
x1

crocodile eyes
black felt
x2

tiger nose
black felt
x1

tiger eye
yellow felt
x2

crocodile nostril
black felt
x2

mole eye
black felt
x2

moose nostril
black felt
x2

mole foot
pink felt
x2

length of owl eyebrows
in scrap yarn
x6

owl beak
yellow felt
x3

pheasant leg
grey felt
x2

owl inside of eye
black felt
x6

owl eye
grey felt
x6

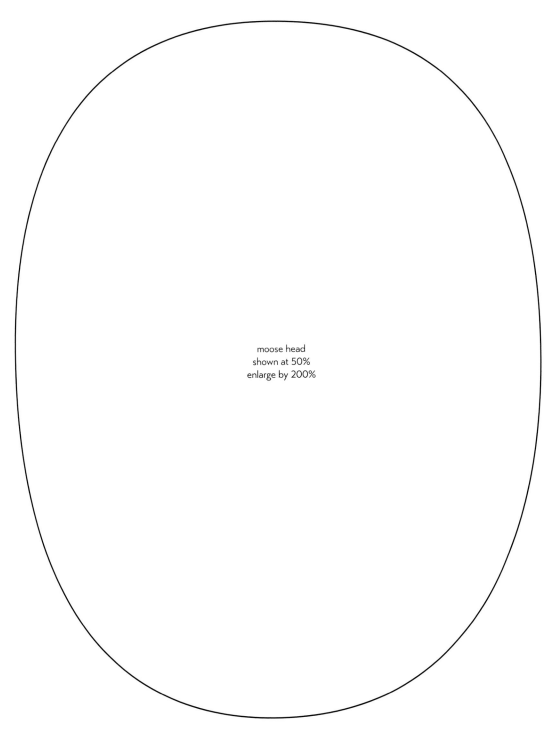

moose head
shown at 50%
enlarge by 200%

ABOUT THE AUTHOR

Louise Walker is a London-based designer recognized for her animal creations and photo series 'Woolly Heads'. Since launching Sincerely Louise in June 2013, her work has been featured in publications including *Tatler*, the *Daily Mail* and the *Sunday Express*. She has been commissioned by Boden, Phileas Fog, *Crafty Magazine* and even a few celebrities. Children and adults alike love her work.

Whilst studying Commercial Photography at the Arts University Bournemouth Louise learned to knit. She caught the craft bug and it quickly became a big part of her work before taking over her life. Louise is a full-time designer and maker, and she can usually be found knitting foxes, dying yarn and watching vast amounts of television in her studio.

ACKNOWLEDGMENTS

I would like to thank everybody who has helped and supported me during the creation of this book. My parents for their continued encouragement and ability to listen to me talk about yarn for hours. Nanny Pam for her inspirational knitted gifts; you'll always be my knitting hero. The rest of my family deserves a big 'thank you' too, for always being so amazing, especially Granddad Colin.

A very special 'thank you' goes to Pete, who kept me company and made many a dinner during the long hours of knitting. I'm grateful for all of the trips to craft shops you accompanied me on as well as your honest feedback. The help you gave truly makes the book what it is. I would also like to thank Rue who joined us in those nights of laughter and who introduced me to *The Rocky Horror Picture Show* whilst I made the Owl Tea Cosy (and various other projects when we watched it again!).

I would also like to thank all of the yarn companies who offered their support; because of you the book features some of the most beautiful yarns I've ever worked with.

Thank you Sarah for making this opportunity a reality. It has truly been the most exciting time of my career. I would also like to thank Harriet for her wonderful help and comments, Emma for her continued support and hard work on the book, Lizzy for her incredible text editing and Anna and Sarah for all their work on the book.

A big 'thank you' goes to the team who helped create the amazing photos seen in the book, especially Ben, who worked day in and out with me creating the shots, sourcing everything we needed, building sets, art directing and being constantly by my side over the days we were taking the images. I never thought I'd be shooting anything for the book, but I'm so happy it was the photos and not my winter scarf!

Finally I would like to thank all of my online friends and followers. You are an amazing community providing support across the social networks. I hope I have inspired you as much as you have inspired me and I can't wait to see your creature creations!

SUPPLIERS

Amber Paradise
www.amberparadise.com

Beads Unlimited
www.beadsunlimited.co.uk

Bergere De France
www.bergeredefrance.co.uk

Brooklyn Tweed
www.brooklyntweed.com

Craft Bits
www.craftbits.co.uk

Drops Design
www.garnstudio.com

Erika Knight
www.erikaknight.co.uk

Force 4
www.force4.co.uk

Garthenor
www.organicpurewool.co.uk

Jamieson & Smith
www.shetlandwoolbrokers.co.uk

John Lewis
www.johnlewis.com

Katia Fun fur
www.modernknitting.co.uk

Malabrigo
www.malabrigoyarn.com

Minerva Crafts
www.minervacrafts.com

Robin
www.rkmwools.co.uk

Rowan
www.knitrowan.com

Sincerely Louise
www.sincerelylouise.co.uk

Stitch Craft Create
www.stitchcraftcreate.co.uk

Stylecraft
www.stylecraft-yarns.co.uk

Texere Yarns
www.texere-yarns.co.uk

Wool and the Gang
www.woolandthegang.com

INDEX

A DAVID & CHARLES BOOK
© F&W Media International, Ltd 2014

David & Charles is an imprint of F&W Media International, Ltd
Brunel House, Forde Close, Newton Abbot, TQ12 4PU, UK

F&W Media International, Ltd is a subsidiary of F+W Media, Inc
10151 Carver Road, Suite #200, Blue Ash, OH 45242, USA

Text and Designs © Louise Walker 2014
Layout and Photography © F&W Media International, Ltd 2014

First published in the UK and USA in 2014

A catalogue record for this book is available from the British Library.

ISBN-13: 978-1-4463-0453-2 paperback
ISBN-10: 1-4463-0453-1 paperback

Printed in the USA by RR Donnelley USA:
F&W Media International, Ltd
Brunel House, Forde Close, Newton Abbot, TQ12 4PU, UK

10 9 8 7 6 5 4 3

Acquisitions Editor: Sarah Callard
Editor: Emma Gardner
Assistant Editor: Harriet Butt
Project Editor: Elizabeth Kingston
Design Manager: Sarah Clark
Photographer: Louise Walker and Ben Swailes
Production Manager: Beverley Richardson

F+W Media publishes high quality books on a wide range of subjects.
For more great book ideas visit: www.stitchcraftcreate.co.uk